G000134831

A SAILMATE BOOK

RUNNING AGROUND
& GETTING AFLOAT

—————— J Schult ——————

ADLARD COLES NAUTICAL
London

This edition published in 1994 by Adlard Coles Nautical
an imprint of A & C Black (Publishers) Ltd 35 Bedford Row,
London WC1R 4JH

Copyright © Klasing & Co, GmbH, Bielefeld 1994
Copyright © English language text
Adlard Coles Nautical 1994

ISBN 0-7136-3896-6

All rights reserved. No part of this publication
may be reproduced in any material form (including
photocopying or storage in any medium by electronic
means and whether or not transiently or incidentally
to some other use of this publication) without the prior
written permission of the copyright owner.

A CIP catalogue record for this book is available from
the British Library.

Translated from the German edition, *Festkommen und
Abbringen Stranden und Bergen.*

Text set in 11/12pt Century Schoolbook by
Falcon Graphic Art Limited, Wallington, Surrey.
Printed and bound in Great Britain by
The Cromwell Press, Melksham, Wiltshire.

Contents

Be prepared for running aground

Earlier in my sailing life in Denmark, running aground and getting afloat was part of the daily routine; almost a more frequent occurrence than coming alongside or leaving a berth! The explanation is simple; the small cruisers used in those days generally had no inboard engine. It was therefore necessary to make numerous short tacks up the long and narrow dredged channels in the shallow waters leading to the river Schlei or similar areas of the southern Danish sea. When entering relatively small harbours under sail, one was sometimes forced to overstand the borders of the dredged channels in order to save another laborious tack. However, running aground rarely led to emergencies requiring outside help, due to the alertness of the helmsman and crew and the correct procedures quickly carried out.

Nowadays, these skills of self-help seem to have diminished because cruisers can run up narrow channels or into narrow harbours under power if the wind is on the nose – just start up the engine and drive the boat like a car up past buoys and piles towards the mooring. So if a boat does run aground it is often totally unexpected and the surprised and unprepared crew may waste precious minutes by doing nothing. A boat, which is at first just scraping gently over the bottom, may be put into an increasingly dangerous situation. Merely touching bottom should never become critical, as long as the entire crew is aware of both the dangers of getting stuck and is also familiar with a rapid freeing procedure.

The likelihood of touching bottom can never be excluded in shallow waters even when using an echo sounder. Becoming fast aground can happen anywhere; in rivers, near coasts, in tidal waters when entering small harbours – even the most careful navigation in areas with moving sandbanks does not preclude the risk.

1

Other causes of running aground may be: a careless crew, incorrect estimation of wind, tide and sea state, navigational errors due to fog or rain, damaged sails or rudder and last, but not least, being swept away due to engine failure.

An experienced skipper will regard touching bottom and getting afloat again as routine a manoeuvre as tacking, gybing, mooring and anchoring. He should be aware that indecisiveness in the crew's reactions, wrong tactics after touching bottom, loss of time or inertia can lead to a situation whereby the boat cannot be freed through self help and outside help (often at significant cost) is required. A simple case of being stuck can lead to stranding and sometimes even to loss of the boat.

Running aground under sail

This chapter describes how to react correctly in different situations when running aground and which procedure should be taken. The basic rule when running aground under sail is always: *Release all sheets immediately!*

If a yacht runs aground when sailing to windward or on a reach, it normally becomes stuck at an angle because it was sailing at a heeled angle due to the force of the wind on the sail. She will right herself after all the sheets have been released and her draught will automatically increase. This will act as a brake and stop her being forced further away from deep safe water.

If the sails are allowed to remain filled after the keel has touched with the sheets pulled in (as is often recommended in order to get afloat) the yacht heels further over and reduces the draught. This will result in the boat sliding further on to the shoal, increasing the area of ground contact which will make the recovery of the boat more difficult.

Running aground on a windward shoal

Running aground on a windward shoal always happens on a windward or beam reach course and often occurs when tacking into a narrow channel. The keel hits the obstruction at a narrow angle. When the boat comes to a standstill the apparent wind (stronger than the true wind during sailing and also from a more forward angle) will die abruptly and be felt further aft, ie it will veer aft.

Because of this, the mainsheet should be released until the main flaps loosely. Strong wind and waves are sometimes sufficient to push the boat away from the edge of a shoal into deeper water. It often helps to transfer the weight of the crew to the stern so the weight is taken off the bow. The required turn to leeward can be achieved by backing the foresail (see Fig 1). If necessary, this manoeuvre can be assisted by using the engine on half power astern.

Whether it is useful to position a crew member on the shrouds in order to heel the boat needs to be decided according to the situation; because the direction of the keel still points towards the shoal and a backed foresail does not necessarily mean that the boat will turn. It is initially better to push the stranded yacht into and through the wind (see Fig 2), instead of pushing her to leeward. Because of the relatively short fin keel in relation to the hull length, most modern fin keelers can be swung from one side to another like a pivot which means they can turn about 50° around their own axis in the direction of the wind with little difficulty.

On bigger boats, the spinnaker boom can be used as a lever.

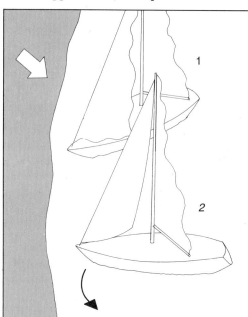

Fig 1 When the boat turns to port it inevitably fills the mainsail (position 2) because the boom can only be let out to a certain point until it becomes obstructed by the shrouds.

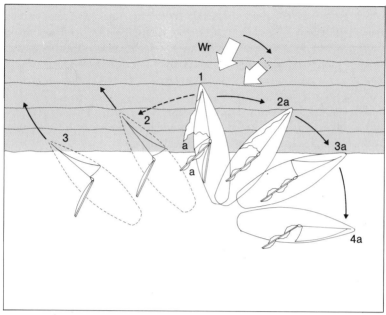

Fig 2 If we run on to an obstruction on a windward course (position 1), the sail is not affected by the direction and strength of the relative or apparent wind (Wr) but by the atmospheric or true wind (Wa) which comes more aft and is less strong. Getting afloat may be achieved (albeit incorrectly) by keeping the sheets in place for a moment in order to heel the boat, back the foresail (2) and release the main so that the boat pushes off (3) with a turn. A quick glance at the diagram reveals that this theoretical suggestion is not very useful in practice as it causes the yacht to become more firmly aground. In reality, the main will inevitably continue to fill whilst the boat continues turning to leeward again, regardless of any efforts to keep it into the wind with its sheets released. Even if the foresail is backed as in position 2, the boat will not turn but will develop sail power (position 3) to windward and move forward. If this situation occurs, the main and foresail sheets must be released immediately (position 1a) and the boat pushed into the wind by using a boat hook or other aids (position 2a). Now the main can flap loosely and with the foresail backed at the right moment, it will turn the bow sharply to leeward (position 3a). The boat continues to turn when the foresail is tacked (position 4a) and simultaneously starts moving to leeward into clear water. Only then is the mainsail allowed to fill and can be trimmed.

Smaller boats may use a boathook which, in this case, is put into the water on the port side of the bow. If the obstruction is less than 1.25 metres a crew member in the water with his back to the boat may ease the boat off but he or she must wear a lifejacket and also a safety harness with a lifeline attached to the boat. It often happens that a boat pushed free this way drifts so quickly into deeper water that the helper (especially when the boat is undermanned) has no chance of catching up with it, so great care must be taken with this option.

Once the yacht is on the other (starboard) tack the foresail is backed and the wind pushes her safely sideways and then forwards back into deeper water. Even if the boat should turn to windward for a brief moment, the edge of the obstruction will be further away than if the boat lies on a port tack.

If the wind direction is at 90° to the edge of the obstruction (Fig 3) and the boat runs aground on the same windward course, it can be freed on the same tack in light or strong winds. In order to maintain the turning momentum away from the edge of the obstruction, the main needs to be freed off until there is no pressure on it when the foresail is backed.

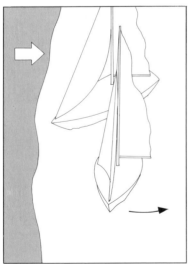

Fig 3

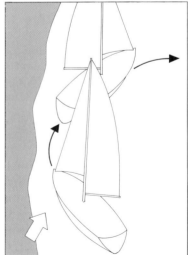

Fig 4

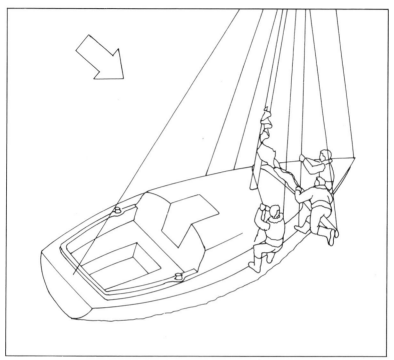

Fig 5

If the boat runs on to a windward obstruction whilst reaching (Fig 4) it might help if the helmsman reacts quickly by throwing the helm hard over, ie gybing the boat quickly by altering course towards the deeper water.

If the gybe is unsuccessful, all sheets need to be released immediately and the sails taken down. When slightly touching the bottom to windward it is probably not necessary to steady the boat on that position. Instead, the boat should be heeled to leeward as far as possible by using the weight of the crew so that the draught is reduced and the boat can drift to leeward back into deeper water (Fig 5). In most cases, it is sufficient to improvise spontaneous heeling by letting crew members lean out at the shrouds. Please note that if the boom is used as a lever, the topping lift is often not strong enough to support the

7

weight of a person in foul weather gear and seaboots. The person riding on the boom should therefore support his body-weight by putting one foot on the gunwale and only lifting the other leg outside the boat as far as possible. The boathook or spinnaker boom can also be used to push the boat off the obstruction.

Another suggestion is to push the boat off physically but the person in the water should wear deck shoes (even in fine weather) which offer a better grip and also protect the feet. The crew member should wear a lifejacket and stay connected to the boat by a safety line with a safety harness to enable boarding safely and quickly once the yacht is afloat.

Getting afloat from a leeward shoal in onshore winds

If a boat starts to run aground on a leeward shoal whilst sailing on a beam reach (Fig 6), the sails should be taken down

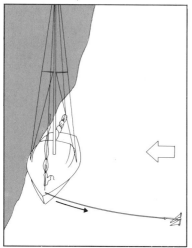

Fig 6

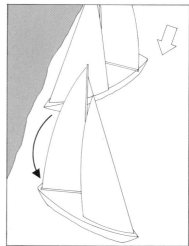

Fig 7

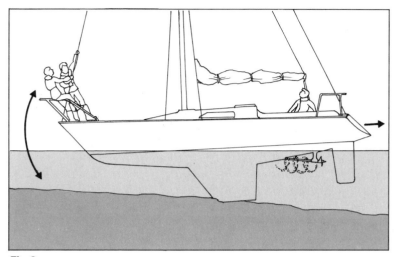

Fig 8

immediately and stowed securely so they cannot be damaged or get in the way. At the same time, the second anchor or kedge should be dropped in order to stop the boat from being carried further on to the obstruction ie slow her down from drifting on to it with the inevitable swell. If the depth of the water is less than 2 metres, the secured anchor warp should generally be let out for about 15 metres so the kedge can get a firm grip and not drag. However, make sure that the anchor warp is long enough; a short warp will not prevent a grounded yacht from moving further to leeward. It is common knowledge that anchors can only hold if the warp is about 6 to 7 times the measurement of the water depth. Once secure, the kedge prevents the boat from being lifted and pushed further away from the edge of the deep water. This technique applies to a wind direction of 90° to a leeward obstruction and also in onshore winds with slight angles to the edge of the shoal.

The only way to avoid an obstruction, before the boat grounds and comes to a complete standstill, is to throw the helm hard over and gybe with a course alteration of at least 90°. This can only be done if she sails on a downwind course

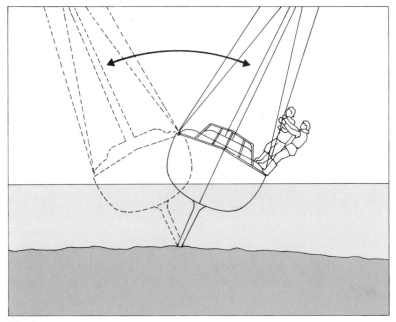

Fig 9

(Fig 7) and the shoal is adjacent to a clear deep water channel. One can try bringing the boat into deeper water by using the engine if the seabed is firm and only gradually slopes upwards. This is done by positioning the crew on the bow (Fig 8) in order to lift the aft section of the keel and alternatively using the engine in 'half' and 'full' power astern.

If this procedure fails because the keel is wedged too deeply into the surrounding sand, one can try to free the boat by alternatively heeling her from one side to the other (Fig 9) or by using the crew to continuously shift their weight from stern to bow. This procedure can be used successfully in tidal waters and does not need to be rushed if the tide is coming in. No time should be wasted though when the tide is going out and you should be careful about weight distribution on the boat. On small cruisers in particular, the crew's weight represents a large proportion of the displacement, but even though two or

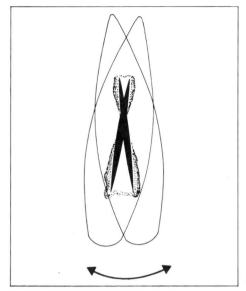

Fig 10

three crew may shift their weight to the bow in order to lift the stern, the draught of the boat remains unchanged. If these crew, each dressed in lifejacket, safety harness and safety line step from the bow into the water, the boat will return to its normal position but it will be lighter by about 200 to 300 kg. Its displacement will then be reduced by about 10 to 15%, depending on the size of the boat. Reducing the draught by a few centimetres can make a remarkable difference. If you resort to this tactic always hang out a boarding ladder or bight of rope at the bow so the people can quickly step aboard once the boat is freed!

The advantage of a short keeled boat is that it is easy to turn around on its longitudinal axis. Long keeled boats tend to dig themselves into the sand because each turn creates a 'sand dune' on either side of the keel (Fig 10) which makes it more difficult to get back afloat.

If all efforts to get afloat remain unsuccessful, you will need to row out the anchor in the dinghy and try kedging off by hauling on the anchor rope (see page 22–3).

High and dry in a motor boat

If a heavy motor boat or long keeled yacht runs aground, the propeller and the shaft are protected by the skeg so that the fixed rudder cannot easily be damaged but getting afloat will be time consuming, especially if the skipper is single handed (Fig 11). In order to get the boat free he has to work outside the boat and should wear deck shoes, safety harness and safety line; the operation's timing will be crucial if the tide is ebbing!

If driving the boat alternately forwards and astern, and heeling her and running forward and aft does not alter the situation, the skipper should secure the anchor warp at the stern and drop the anchor over the bow to prevent the boat from drifting away when she comes afloat (Fig 11B). He should also remember to attach the swim ladder at the stern to allow him to climb back on board; he may end up exhausted and there will be no one else available to assist him.

If the skipper cannot free the boat by pushing in the direction of the keel, he needs to turn it. To do this he must to lift and push the boat simultaneously, ie lift the bow whilst turning (Fig 11C). The simplest way to do this is to push the boat up with a straight back instead of trying to pull it. A turn of 90° (Fig 11D) can be sufficient to free the boat depending on the position and type of obstruction. Once the boat has turned 180° the skipper should climb on board using the swim ladder and shift any movable weight towards the bow to help to free the stern. Then he should haul the anchor and push the boat from the foredeck into deeper water by using the boathook. If the stern remains stuck, the skipper should go on to the foredeck and use his bodyweight, to create a seesaw action which dips the foredeck into the water and consequently lifts the stern off the obstruction. Once you are afloat and you know that there is a fair depth of water in front of the obstruction it is best to keep the boat anchored until you have checked the

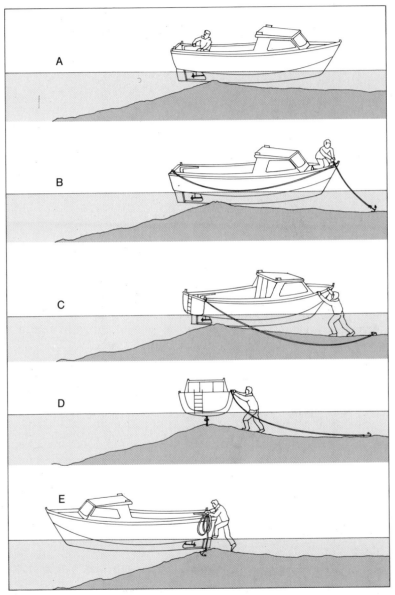

Fig 11

hull, engine and propeller. If you find any damage, it is safer to anchor on the obstruction and remain there rather than let the boat drift away to an unknown destination in deep water.

Obviously, all these tips to free a grounded motor boat only apply if the engine has been unable to get the boat afloat or the engine cannot be used because of possible damage to the propeller.

Using ground tackle to get afloat

Even if all the procedures previously mentioned have proved unsuccessful, a small crew, even on a large cruiser or motor boat, has every chance of getting afloat again in almost all weather conditions by using ground tackle, depending on the state of the tide.

Anchor types

A boat should be equipped with at least one heavyweight bower (main) anchor and another lighter anchor. The main anchor is

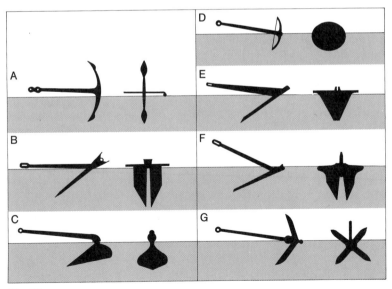

Fig 12

generally dropped from the bow and the secondary anchor or kedge, from the stern. This two-anchor technique is often practised in crowded anchorages where the lack of space makes it necessary to reduce the swinging circle.

When an anchor is used to free a boat from an obstruction, the anchor is put under immense strain and should possess a strong holding ability which is not just dependent on its weight but also on its type of flukes. This aspect, therefore, should be considered when selecting an anchor from the wide range on offer. Fig 12 shows the holding ability of various common anchor types in relation to one another:

The *fisherman* (A) and the *grapnel* anchor (G) clearly show that their flukes are extremely narrow and therefore only 50% of their shape is used as actual holding power. These two anchor types offer little resistance against the immense tension required for the recovery procedure and break out quickly.

The *plough* anchor (CQR) (C) is the most commonly used type on cruising boats and its surface area is very similar to that of the mud or *mushroom* anchor (D) which was used on fire boats but it bites deeper into the seabed especially when put under strong tension. The *Danforth* anchor (B) compared to the *delta* (E) has the advantage of being more flexible and having two double flukes.

The area of the *d'Hone* anchor (F) is nearly equal to that of the Danforth anchor but slightly broader and therefore more favourable for recovering a boat.

According to some sailing books it seems that most boats only run aground on clean fine sand in which almost any anchor holds and where the seabed is visible in clear water so that the anchor can be dropped or, if possible, walked out comfortably. Unfortunately, the reality is slightly different! One needs to be aware of the type of ground when the anchor is laid out by dinghy or walked out (Fig 13). Most anchors have a reasonable holding ability in firm sand or mud (A) but should also be fairly heavy if they are to bite firmly and hold safely at the onset.

On rocks (B) the holding ability of the anchor depends on its weight. A lightweight anchor does not bite at all because it drags over the ground even when under slight strain. If it gets

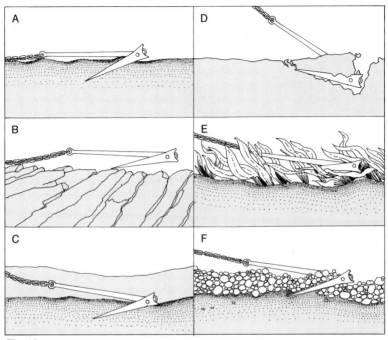

Fig 13

stuck in the crevice of a rock it might enable you to recover the boat but there is the danger of losing the anchor if it cannot be hauled up.

In mud, which generally lies above firm sand (C), the anchor normally drags over the bottom for quite a while before it bites into the solid ground and holds. If a boat has run aground in a muddy seabed, you need to run out the anchor as far as possible. This might require all spare warps.

Clay or loam (D) are an excellent holding ground where even lightweight anchors with large flukes hold extremely well. Seagrass and seaweed (E) make recovery extremely difficult because it hinders the anchor from reaching the actual seabed. In most cases, the anchor will drag unless it can bite firmly into the bottom. If small stones or pebbles (F) are lying on top of a coarser bottom, the anchor requires considerable weight in order to dig into the pebbles and reach the firm substrate.

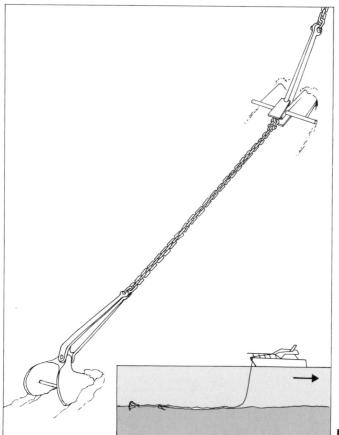

Fig 14

Backed anchors and tripping lines

To increase the holding power under the immense strain of recovering a yacht, one can use two anchors 'backing up each other'. First, the smaller and lighter anchor is dropped, safely secured to the head of the main anchor, with 3 to 5 metres of chain (Fig 14) or warp. Then the anchor warp is led from the shank of the main anchor back to the boat. Both anchors hold without interfering with each other. If the main anchor is in danger of breaking free because of too much strain, the small anchor will help to stabilise it by adding extra grip.

Sometimes the anchor shank lifts during the recovery procedure; for example, if it is used as a fixed point to careen the boat by sheering the recovery line over the masthead to the deck. In this case the anchor becomes a lever which breaks the grip of the fluke and causes it to be lifted out of the seabed. To avoid this, you should try to lower additional ballast to a point between the chain and the anchor head. This can consist of a special anchor weight or any other suitable heavy item (Fig 15), for example looping the unused chain of the smaller anchor into a bundle and lowering it to the anchor with a warp which is secured to a large shackle (A). Another solution is to collect heavy items from the boat and pack them into a tool sack which is tied together at the top (B). Attaching these additional weights to a warp means that they can be lifted before the anchor itself is hauled up.

You should also consider attaching a buoyed tripping line (Fig 16) to the anchor when using it for getting back afloat. If the boat has to leave quickly due to the wind and sea state, once it is afloat the anchor can be slipped and the boat sailed to a safe anchorage, or run into a nearby harbour or allowed to drift whilst the crew is occupied with other important jobs.

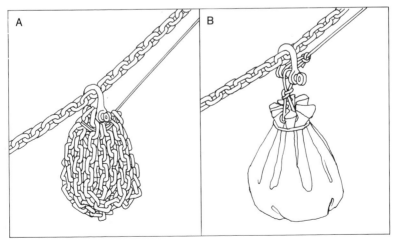

Fig 15

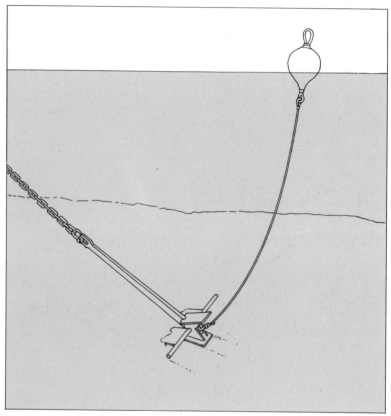

Fig 16

Later on, the anchor line can be recovered with the help of the marked tripping line.

Bollard hitch

The warps used for getting a boat afloat are under an immense strain and the knots and fastenings to cleats or bollards pull very tightly when under load for long periods of

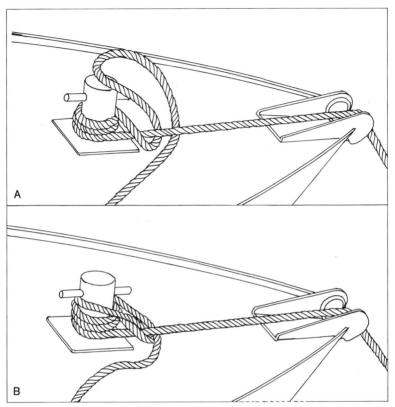

Fig 17

time. The normal methods of tying off on cleats or tying knots such as half hitches or bowlines around bollards are not very suitable because the warp tends to jam and becomes difficult to release under pressure. This prevents the crew from unfastening the warp quickly once the yacht is afloat and jammed turns also make it difficult to give more slack if required. This is why the 'bollard hitch' should be used for securing the recovery line or anchor chain (Fig 17) to a fitting, regardless of whether it is a straight bollard or one with a cross piece. Put two or three turns around the bollard, make a loop with the loose part, feed it under the line and put it over the bollard

(A). Then, the loose part (B) is pulled through. This knot can also be used on a cleat if the crossbar is of sufficient height. No matter how much strain is on the line, it will always be possible to release it completely or take off the last loop in order to feed out more slack if necessary.

Laying out an anchor by dinghy or by swimming

Tenders are now often standard equipment on cruisers. If you use anchorages for overnight stays or for swimming, you will probably have a tender ready on deck or in davits so it can be used for trips to the shore for visits or shopping. People who mainly choose harbours for their day trip destinations usually carry an inflatable dinghy stowed on deck or down below. Such dinghies are sometimes intended for use in an emergency instead of a liferaft.

A dinghy is indispensable for recovering a grounded boat; it can be used to lay the anchor out far enough away from the boat to reach deep water. It is never possible to 'throw the anchor far into the water' as some textbooks incorrectly suggest, because a light anchor, that can be thrown a dozen metres away from the yacht, will not take the strain of recovering the boat. Similarly, heavy anchors which plunge into the water a few metres away from the hull do not provide you with sufficient distance for a useful recovery. Obviously, this does not apply to the stern anchor, ie kedge, which should be dropped when the yacht has run aground in order to prevent the boat from drifting into further danger. The stern anchor is used to secure the boat in position so that the main anchor can later be used for the actual recovery in the best deep water position.

For recovering the boat by laying out the anchor by dinghy one needs to use the longest line available. Attach another line (about a third of the length of the recovery warp) between the yacht and the recovery warp; the slack can be secured to a fit-

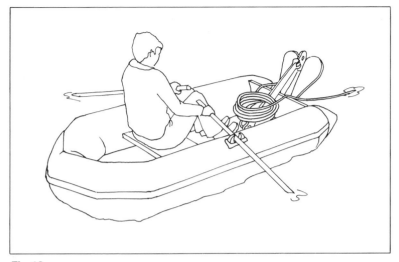

Fig 18

ting on the foredeck once the anchor has caught. The anchor warp should be thick enough to be gripped comfortably by hand but should also be sufficiently thin and flexible to be pulled through a block or put around a winch.

When the dinghy is ready to lay out the anchor, it should be brought alongside the yacht. The anchor should be balanced on the stern ready for dropping. The anchor chain is flaked out and the warp is coiled in the stern so that it can run freely as the dinghy is rowed out; the attached connecting line is coiled on top (Fig 18).

If no dinghy is available or it is not usable you may need to swim out the anchor. Some means of flotation will be needed to support the anchor; several fenders can be tied together and the anchor attached with a slip bend or rip cord (Fig 19). This emergency 'anchor pontoon' should be swum out with a second line secured to it (in addition to the recovery warp which has to be let out from the yacht). Once the anchor is dropped, this second line can be hauled in to bring the fenders and the swimmer back aboard. The job of swimming out the anchor can be made a little easier (depending on the distance he has

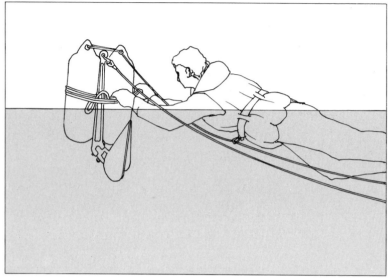

Fig 19

to swim) if fenders are connected to the anchor warp every 10 or 15 m so that the warp does not sink too deeply. This is an extremely tiring swim and should only be attempted by a very strong, fit swimmer wearing a life jacket.

From my experience, I think there should be a towing warp of 100 metres length onboard which can be divided into two ends of about 40 to 60 m.

Nylon (polyamide) makes a suitable towing warp as it is very strong: a three-strand 15 mm polyester rope has a breaking strain of 4100 kg compared with a three-strand polyester rope of the same diameter which has a 3180 kg breaking strain; a 15 mm polypropylene rope has only a 2800 kg breaking strain. Alternatively, you can use 12 mm kevlar rope which is sheathed in easy-grip polyester and is extremely strong, though expensive. The disadvantage to kevlar is that it is less suitable for making small turns or attaching lines with knots.

The best connecting line for hauling in the end of the recovery warp (which should be able to sink quickly to the seabed when laid out by dinghy) is a buoyant warp (polypropylene)

which lies on the surface of the sea and is therefore not short-
ened by looping down. I use my 10 mm lifeline made from 8-
ply polypropylene-multifil from its runner on the stern. With a
maximum pulling power of 1200 DAN (Kilonewtons per sq m)
it is strong enough to haul in the recovery warp.

Getting afloat by using an anchor

The crew can provide enough trimming weight to heel the boat
by swinging the boom forwards (with the kicking strap) or
abaft (with the mainsheet). However, to prevent damage,
attach at least one more halyard (next to the topping lift) to

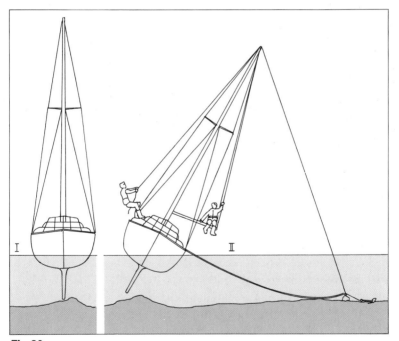

Fig 20

the end of the boom (see Fig 20). Then the anchor is rowed out into deep water so that the heeling angle lifts the keel from the seabed. There is a problem if only one crew is available to heel the boat and there is only one anchor as this will be needed as a fixed point to heel it and also for getting afloat again (Fig 20 II). In this situation the spinnaker halyard must also be attached to the anchor shank before the anchor is dropped. The shank itself should be weighed down with additional weights (see Fig 15) so that the anchor cannot break out once the direction of pull changes from horizontal to vertical.

Wherever a line is used from anchor to masthead, one should never take the main halyard or the genoa halyard because these lines can easily slip off the lead at the masthead even in slight heeling angles, thus making the continuation of work impossible. During this procedure, the anchor warp itself should not be led to the bow but amidships to a pulley near the mast or to the shrouds because otherwise the boat will turn bow to anchor when the anchor warp is pulled and the heeling effect will be lost. Actually, this procedure, using one anchor, indicates why a second anchor is indispensable, especially when the yacht is shorthanded. One of the two anchors can be dropped abeam of the boat to heel it whilst the other anchor is laid in the direction of the deep water to free it. These methods are explained as follows.

Freeing a boat using two anchors

If all spontaneous efforts to free the boat have been unsuccessful (see pages 3–8) and the position of the yacht aground held by the stern anchor unchanged, the main anchor should be rowed as far away to windward as possible into deep water (Fig 21) so it digs in deeply and securely. Now the boat is heeled, not only by using the crew on the main boom, but also by using ballast which is attached to the boom and swung out as far as possible to one side. This side is preferably the deep

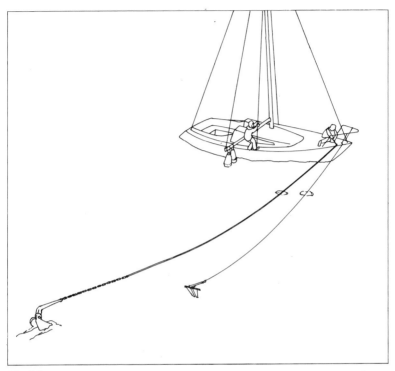

Fig 21

water side as it makes it easier for the keel to slide off. With this procedure, do remember to attach the main halyard or even another halyard next to the topping lift on the end of the boom. The best heeling effect is achieved if one person sits in the bosun's chair (which is hung from the end of the boom) with another person on his lap. The second or third person can also ride on the end of the boom and hold on to the topping lift. These 'trimming weights' are swung out by using a bull pendant from the end of the boom to the bow. Towards the stern the diagonal position of the boom is held by the main sheet. You should make sure that the people hanging or sitting on the boom are absolutely safe as it can take a considerable amount of time to release them from their position after the boat is freed; the first priority when the boat is afloat is to prevent it from running aground again.

When you are in a position to haul in the anchor, you need to decide whether to do it from the normal hauling position at the bow, which is the shortest way to the windlass, or whether it should be hauled from amidships in the mast/shroud area from where the end of the anchor warp can be led to the bow and the windlass. Alternatively, one can use the sheet winches near the cockpit. More power is produced with an emergency working tackle (see Fig 26) which is indispensable especially when recovering larger yachts.

If the heeling effect is insufficient, the stern anchor can be hauled in and rowed out a few boat lengths further away into the deep water. Then the anchor warp is put around the mast, pulled up until it reaches the crosstrees and attached as described in Fig 22A. The line rove halfway between both fixed points is secured with a stopper knot (Fig 22B). It helps to

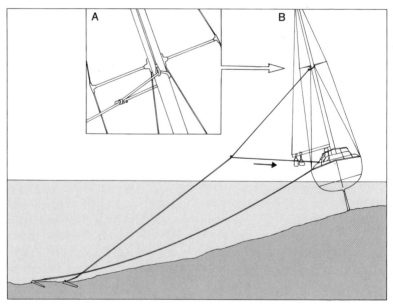

Fig 22

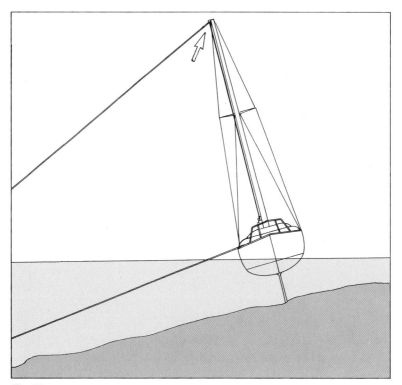

Fig 23

increase the boat's heeling angle and therefore prevents the anchor shank from being lifted out of the seabed because the angle at which it is lifted towards the crosstrees (see Fig 20) is smaller.

Attaching the stern anchor warp to a halyard and winding it in through its lead at the masthead (Fig 23) seems sensible at first glance because it gives the impression that the winding as well as the leverage (at the masthead) is very effective. This is incorrect because firstly the mast fittings are not designed to take this amount of strain and secondly the halyards will slip off their fairleads as the heeling effect increases. If somebody does take the risk of trying to free their boat in this way, it should only be done by using the spinnaker halyard which is led

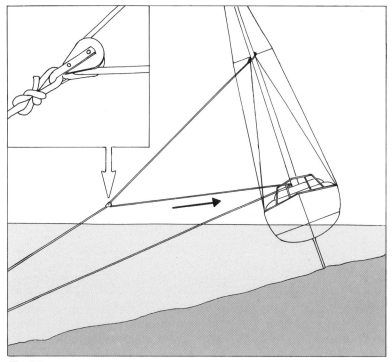

Fig 24

through a separate block of adequate strength at the masthead; experience has shown that the strain can still be too much.

If a strong leading block for 14 mm or (even better) for 16 mm rope is part of the emergency equipment (which can also be used for getting afloat with assistance, see Fig 30) the following method can be used. The block is secured to the anchor warp and the actual 'heeling line' which is made fast to the crosstrees, is led through the pulley down to the deck (Fig 24). The energy saved this way is equivalent to 1:2 but the block needs to be attached far enough away from the boat so that the 'heeling line' from the crosstrees cannot get blocked.

All these methods of trying to free the boat can be made easier by the wash of passing boats. Very often it pays to be patient and use the movement of the sea by asking the crew to

Fig 25

run from the stern to the bow or from port to starboard. You could also try to lighten the boat, ie getting rid of unnecessary weight to reduce the displacement of the yacht. This can be done by shifting water tanks, tool cases, fuel cans and other compact weights into the dinghy and consider other options in order to reduce the draught.

Depending on the shape of the stern, it can also be useful to secure the dinghy under it when the yacht is trimmed down by the bow (Fig 25). If the dinghy is secured partially inflated and only fully inflated afterwards, the increase of volume from 300 to 500 litres can produce another favourable lifting effect especially if it is used at the heaviest and widest part of a light boat.

Adding pulling power by using working tackle

Obviously one will use an existing windlass to free a grounded yacht, but with a reduction of the pulling power by 2:1 it is insufficient to pull a grounded 5 tonne motor sailer from sand into deeper water, even when heeled. If a sheet winch with its relatively small pulling power is used to recover a grounded yacht, one should always attach a working tackle to the anchor warp. This increases the pulling power and also allows the load to be hauled in manually, by use of the windlass or sheet

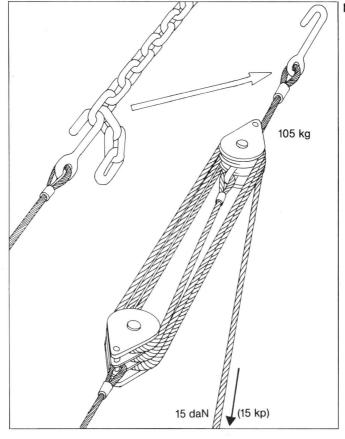

Fig 26

105 kg

15 daN   (15 kp)

winch if no other mechanical aids are available. The main sheet which normally has two double blocks, one with becket and one without, can be used as an emergency working tackle and can produce an energy saving of 1:5 or 1:4 (depending on the direction in which the rope is pulled). It is always risky to use the mainsheet as emergency tackle because if the blocks get damaged due to overloading, they become useless for their usual purpose. In most cases the main sheet is already in use anyway ie for swinging out the boom. One should therefore always carry emergency working tackle which can be used as a spare main sheet as well as for heavy jobs like recovering a grounded yacht. If the tackle is made from durable material and consists of two three-runner blocks with and without becket (Fig 26) it will equal an energy saving of 1:6 or 1:7 depending on the direction of the pull. A strong hook connected to the tackle with a short, strong strop can be hooked into the anchor chain.

The pulling power can be multiplied by using a whip block (a block spliced on to the end of the rope) and winding in the anchor warp on one of the sheet winches: With only 15 DAN strength an ordinary person can achieve a pulling power of

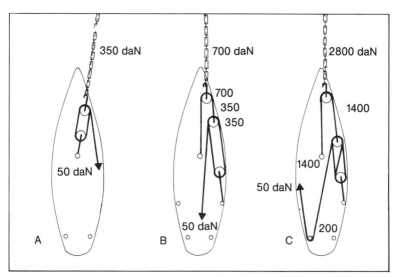

Fig 27

105 DAN which would be necessary to move a mass of 105 kg (Fig 27). This of course is only a tiny part of a grounded cruiser weighing 3000 kg. A strong person using 50 DAN to pull the rope could achieve a load of 350 DAN or shift a much larger percentage of the cruiser weight with 350 kg (Fig 27A).

By using the same amount of strength (50 DAN) this can already be increased to 700 kg if one attaches another strong leading block in front of this working tackle by securing its fixed part to the loose part in the other leading block which is actually a whip block (Fig 27B). Here, the block of the whip block takes a load of 700 DAN and both three runner blocks each 350 DAN. Obviously, the blocks need to be designed to take such strain and they normally are. A small cruiser of about 3 tonnes displacement can always be freed by using such working tackle, whip block and a sheet winch (Fig 27C). First, the block of a whip block is secured with a shackle to the anchor chain, warp or line. The fixed part is (if required, split into two ends) secured to a cleat or to another fixed point on deck; it is questionable whether the mast is suitable for this purpose. The loose part of the whip block leads to the tail block of the working tackle which is safely secured midships or further aft with its fixed part. The loose part of the tackle is then led to one of the sheet winches where it can be winched in. Depending on the type of winch (one speed or two speed), its diameter and its load transmission (from 4:1 to about 40:1), a strong man applying 50 DAN on the winch handle produces a final strength of 2800 DAN and starts moving a cruiser with a displacement of about 2.8 tonnes (depending on the density of the seawater).

Fig 27C displays the distribution of the workload on all fixed and moving parts. One should select at least double the (guaranteed) breaking strength if the working tackle and its additional devices need to be used in this way on a grounded boat. The financial expenditure on these precautions will always be negligible compared to the costs of using outside assistance. Even if the insurance takes on such claims, the loss of the no claims bonus is far higher in financial terms than the cost of a few strong blocks or high performance working tackle.

Getting afloat with outside assistance

If a grounded yacht cannot be recovered with self-help methods and calls another boat to its aid, the other boat is entitled to charge the yacht for the time taken and material expenses (for example the amount of diesel used, use of the engine etc).

Yacht skippers generally quickly come to a low cost agreement between themselves. Crews on working vessels generally demand higher compensation. Bills amounting to four digits are not uncommon for recovering a boat and for this very reason one should first try to get afloat through self-help before involving outside parties.

Legal problems when recovering or salvaging a boat

Individual international legal and insurance regulations for giving assistance and salvage attempt to serve both the interests of the owner of the grounded yacht, and the interests of the owner and skipper of the rescuing boat. When a boat is recovered with outside help, a simple international rule applies: 'No cure, no pay'. This means if a small boat has tried unsuccessfully to recover your yacht for some considerable time through the efforts of its crew, and a substantial amount of diesel has been used, he does so at his own risk. If he gives up and a larger boat with a more powerful engine comes along and frees your boat in a shorter time you will only have to pay for the aid of the latter, ie the successful helper.

You may find yourself in a situation where your boat has sprung a leak after running aground; it could be lying high and dry, in constant danger of being seriously damaged by waves. Therefore it needs to be freed immediately before it becomes a wreck. With this situation costly assistance or even salvage of the yacht is better than allowing the boat to become a total loss because you have refused assistance.

The skipper of the other boat is not always close enough to speak directly to the skipper of the grounded yacht and it is impossible to make a written agreement because one cannot prepare the paperwork and row it back and forth between the two boats. In this case it is sufficient to communicate by VHF and agree on an assistance agreement according to the Lloyds 'Open Form'. After successfully freeing the grounded yacht, the skipper of the rescue boat will make his demands in relation to the value of the rescued property, the risks to his own boat during the freeing process, and to the amount of time taken. Your insurance company will know how to evaluate such demands before accepting and honouring them.

As the skipper of a grounded, endangered yacht you should endeavour to negotiate with the assisting skipper and agree on a fixed amount for the assistance and note:

- Only use your own lines to tow or free the boat.
- Do not let the crew of the other boat come aboard or pass any items for freeing the boat from their boat on to yours. Otherwise, the assistance could turn into a salvage.
- Write the price that has been agreed for the freeing of the yacht and possible towage to the next harbour into your logbook and let someone from your crew who was present at the verbal agreement countersign.
- Log the weather condition, sea state, and names of witnesses for the help and work done by both parties with countersignatures.

Never:
- Talk to the crew of the other boat about the value of the yacht or even inform them about its present value or its insurance value in pounds.
- Refer to the fact that the boat is insured or reveal the name of the insurance company;
- Leave the boat before or during the assistance period or

allow somebody to go across to the helping boat unless the person has to, for example, for medical reasons.

Some insurance companies state that use of your own or foreign lines are irrelevant to the evaluation of cost associated with the assistance received. Despite this, I suggest that if you decide to use other people's equipment (for example, because their lines are stronger) you offer the crew an appropriate amount for its use, prior to assistance commencing. The evaluation of the work performed by other crew should also be realistic. Merchant seamen and fisherman know exactly what they are worth in a situation like this and how to evaluate the cost of their boat per hour and their own hourly rate.

A realistic evaluation is made by calculating an hourly rate equal to that of a foreman for each person taking part, and for the boat a rate equal to that of the hourly rate of a recovery service for your car. The total will roughly equate to the work performed by your helper. This evaluation can be applied to any assisting vessel and crew whether performed by merchant seamen or another yachtsman. These days, a bottle of rum is hardly sufficient unless the other person accepts this tip on a friendly basis. If the yacht is freed quickly and has no damage, one can try to pay the skipper of the other boat in cash by making him a realistic offer. Most people would regard a generous amount of cash paid straight away preferable to a bank cheque for a slightly larger amount which is paid weeks later and will also be subject to tax.

Assistance from other crews

The freeing of a grounded yacht will only run smoothly and quickly and without injuries if the crew of the grounded yacht works in unison with the crew of the assisting boat. It is necessary to agree beforehand on the manoeuvres which are to be carried out. If the boat is only high and dry at around 20 to 30 cm's (which can be seen from the flotation line compared to the water level) the helper can attempt a direct tow (Fig 28). The

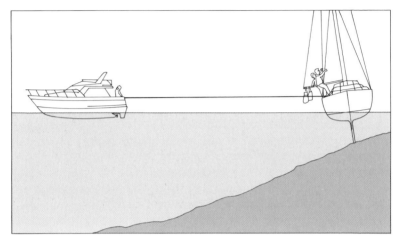

Fig 28

crew of the grounded yacht should then try to heel the boat towards deep water by sitting on the swung-out boom and leaning out, holding on to the shrouds.

You need to agree from the start whether the assisting boat will anchor in deeper water before attempting to free the grounded boat or whether it will remain floating free but under power. If the grounded yacht is to leeward, the helper will in any case hang a fender or some other floating item on the end of a buoyant line which is fed by hand from the stern so it can drift to the grounded yacht. The actual towing warp is then attached to the floating line. The tied off length of the towing warp between the two boats should not be longer than about 3 times the length of the towing boat so it can pull strongly but not jerk the warp with a sudden movement. The towing warp should be attached to the safest point on the grounded yacht – depending on the boat's position – the bow is not always the best fixing point. Whether the boat is freed from the direction of keel or beam must be agreed upon.

It is tempting to tie the towing warp with a bowline around the mast and thus let the towing boat heel the boat whilst the crew uses the anchor warp to try to pull the boat off. However,

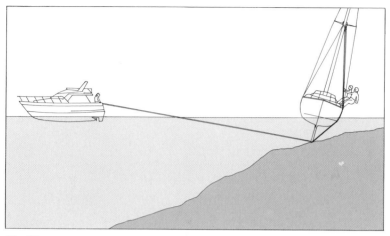

Fig 29

this is quite risky: firstly, the rig is not designed for this purpose, secondly, it is quite difficult and dangerous to handle any lines on the heeled foredeck.

It is better to lead the towing line, which is tied off at the crosstrees, under the hull or under the keel (this method is also suggested if the grounded boat can only be heeled towards the side of the obstruction). This achieves a simultaneous heeling and pulling effect whilst one part of the load is taken by the hull itself (Fig 29).

To take the strain off all possible fastening points, the towing warps can be attached doubled up like a belt in front and abaft the keel, thus using the hull itself as a fixed point for freeing the boat. This method is shown in Fig 43 and also in the photo on page 75 where it is used to free a stranded yacht. The best way is to fasten these lines separately on the towing boat but one can also lead them together to a crow foot. If the towing warps are too short to free the boat, the ends can be tied to the loop of the bowline of the anchor warp which then obviously needs to be strong enough to hold the strain of both towing warps. Another way of increasing the holding power in such a situation is to row out your own anchor, attach a leading block to the end of the towing line (Fig 30) and fasten the leading part of the anchor warp to the motor boat for towing. If

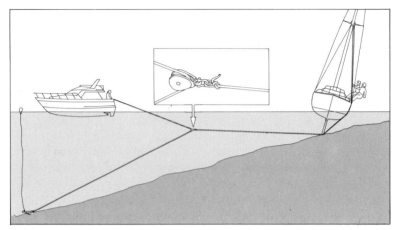

Fig 30

the single block has sufficient holding power, and the anchor is dug firmly into the seabed, even a small motor boat will be able to double its performance.

Such manoeuvres are carried out at only half power. The thrust from a motor boat from stationary to half-power is greater than when it is running at full power with the prop operating at higher revs.

Attaching recovery lines to free a boat

If a motor sailor or a motorboat helps to free a grounded sailing yacht by using its powerful engine, careful thought must be given to the attachment points for the towing warps on both vessels. Hardly any yacht these days is equipped with cleats that are strong enough to take these immense strains. In most cases it is even insufficient to distribute the load on both boats on to two separate cleats. The success or failure of a manoeuvre with outside help, therefore, largely depends on the methods chosen for securing the towing warp. The crew of the assisting vessel should fasten a two-ended towing warp on

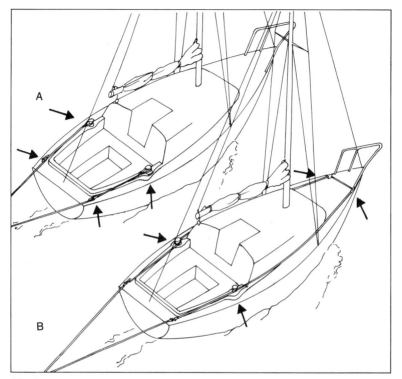

Fig 31

cleats or bollards in the aft section of the boat (Fig 31) and, additionally, wrap it around the sheet winches on either side. A strong cleat on the foredeck or the base of the windlass might also be used for attaching the towing warp. In this case, several turns of the warp should be put around the sheet winches in order to distribute the load evenly and take the strain (Fig 31B). The mast is unsuitable as a fixed point for attaching the towing warp unless it is a very sturdy keel stepped mast. It is best to lead the towing warp to the strongest cleat on the foredeck and thence back to the stern. The risk of damaging the cleats can be avoided if the towing warp is led around the complete hull to the bow like a harness.

This method, seen in Fig 32, can also be used for a large

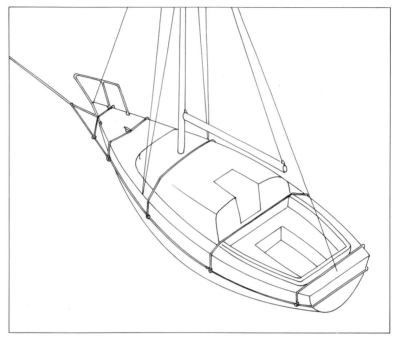

Fig 32

towing cruiser which can have the same problem of where to fasten the towing warp safely. If a motorboat is towing, the crew should lead the towing warp to a point on the stern which lies midships (in direction of the keel). If there is no single strong point in the middle of the stern (as on most boats) to make fast the warp (Fig 33A), one can improvise by attaching short strong lines on each cleat or bollard on either side of the stern and fasten the towing line with a bowline (see Fig 33B). This method of distributing the load on to two cleats is always better than using only one cleat to take the strain (Fig 33C).

A motor yacht can avoid all risks of possible damage to its hull due to overload on its stern cleats if it is fitted with a harness made of longitudinal and diagonal warps, as described in Fig 32 for a towed sailing yacht.

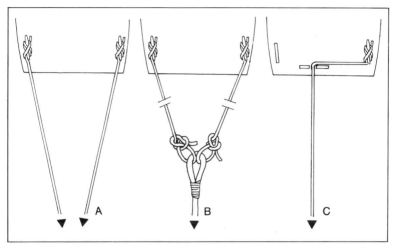

Fig 33

Figures 28 to 30 have shown how to free sailing yachts positioned broadside to obstructions. Figure 33 shows lines attached to the stern by cleats so that the boat can be towed off along the line of the keel. There is, however, another option. Double bollards, winches or other strong fittings on the foredeck can be used. A piece of wood of sufficient length, maybe the boom or the wooden steps can be placed under a forehatch (sufficiently padded to prevent chafing) with the towing line attached ready for slipping (Fig 34A). The strain is now transferred on to the complete hull and no deck fitting is under direct strain. The sheet winches can be another option as attachments for the towing line to the boat (Fig 34B) but in order to avoid too much vertical pull it should be led to the foredeck and tied off on cleats on the bow. As a last resort, or in an emergency, the towing line can be placed around the root of a bilge or fin keel (see Fig 43 whereby this method is used to tow a stranded boat back into deep water). This method will probably require a crew member to dive under the boat to attach the rope and the skipper needs to decide whether this procedure is viable depending on the circumstances, as there should be no risk to the crew.

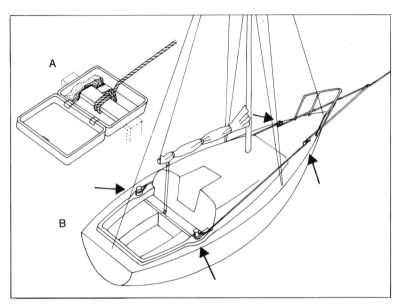

Fig 34

If a heavy motor sailer needs to be freed from an obstruction, the warp on the tow vessel needs to be rigged as in shown in Fig 32 by attaching it like a harness around the complete hull and securing it from slipping off by attaching safety lines across the deck. Obviously, it will take some time to rig the boat in this way but, if it is done properly, the towing vessel need not suffer any damage to deck fittings because the total strain is distributed equally from stern to bow.

Towing with steel cables

If a commercial vessel helps free a grounded yacht or tows her in, it generally uses tow ropes made from fibre strands whose diameter, breaking strain and ease of use are in proportion to the size of the yacht. Because of bad experiences with fibre hawsers breaking, sea rescue boats nearly always use steel hawsers for towing or salvaging yachts.

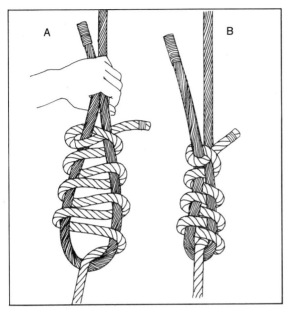

Fig 35 Make a loop with the steel hawser (A) and hold it together with one hand, now put the towing warp into the loop and make several turns going alternatively over and under each side of the loop. The knot will tighten when strained (B).

If a crew is expected to use a steel hawser, which is quite risky to handle, it is best done by tying off (single or double turns sheered) the strongest rope on the firmest point from where it is led through the fairlead on the bow or attached to the bow and tied together with the steel hawser as shown in Fig 35A.

According to the regulations governing safety at work, work gloves need to be worn when working with steel hawsers due to the danger of injury. Note that opening this knot (which remains taut even when the load is taken off) is very difficult in an emergency (Fig 35B). A double sheet bend, which is generally used for tying together two ropes of different sizes, is safer and easier to release. If the steel hawser has a spliced eye, the end of your tow rope can be tied on to it by using a double round turn and two half hitches.

Legal advice

Getting a grounded yacht afloat may not just involve physical strength. If your boat has been freed with outside assistance you also need to be aware of the mountains of legislation which affect you.

In accordance with an international agreement on salvage and assistance in distress, every captain of a vessel is obliged to assist another vessel in peace time as well as in war. This also applies to cases where vessels are grounded. The internationally used word 'assistance' can be interpreted as the support or aid which everybody has to give at sea unless their vessel, crew or passengers are likely to be brought into real danger. For sailors and motor boat skippers this means that if you sight a grounded or stranded yacht you must stop or even anchor (sea and weather conditions permitting), without putting your own boat into danger, in order to investigate the situation and if necessary offer assistance with all the means at your disposal. This can entail simply taking children, injured or incapacitated people aboard, or by lending warps, lines, anchors and other equipment for the boat to free itself. However the loan of equipment must not be to the detriment of your own needs.

In reality, the possibility of a small cruiser giving successful assistance in heavy weather is extremely limited. Yachts which are insufficiently equipped can run into serious danger when trying to rescue another boat, as numerous instances have shown, although they can – if the grounded or stranded boat has no VHF radio or radio telephone – relay messages or distress calls which can be of vital importance.

Personal or technical assistance does not always have to be paid for with money or gifts; the helper may offer assistance in the interests of good seamanship. The skipper of the grounded boat should, if possible, try to establish, before accepting outside help, whether the help is offered free of charge ie from genuine kindness, or whether he will have to pay for the cost of fuel and any damage caused to the assisting boat or if the helper will demand a specific sum for compensation later on depending on the amount of time and help given.

On the other hand, a skipper who sails or motors past a boat that is signalling or calling for help, and perhaps even refuses to lend the grounded vessel the required equipment, can be found guilty of refusing to give assistance in accordance with international regulations. If reported, he will be fined a substantial amount of money. Whether the act of helping to free a grounded yacht or giving a tow is interpreted as 'kindness'; 'rescue of property' or 'technical assistance' can result in legal 'compensation of costs' for a substantial 'assistance payment' as recently decided in an interesting court case.

The German equivalent to the RNLI sued the owner of the small cruiser *Golden Years*, a Sprinta Sport (LOA 7 m, BOA 2.40 m, draught 1.30 m, sail area 29 sq m, displacement 1.3 tonnes, no inboard engine). As reported in the German yachting magazine *Yacht*, the *Golden Years* was presented with a bill in excess of 1808 DM (£723) when it requested a tow into Bremerhaven from a small vessel sailing in the same direction. On her way home the *Golden Years* had become becalmed during a falling tide and was drifting in the shipping lane. The small vessel turned out to be a lifeboat of the German RNLI equivalent which towed the yacht for a while and then handed it over to a larger lifeboat which was on duty, which towed the *Golden Years* into the harbour.

The crew of the *Golden Years* thought they were simply getting a 'lift' but the 'RNLI' charged them 325 DM (£130) per hour for exactly 5.2 hours during the time that both of their boats were 'on duty'. This resulted in a total of 1690 DM (£676) plus 7% VAT ie 1808 DM (£723). The owner was legally obliged to pay. The court confirmed a towage fee of 67 DM (£27) per nautical mile which the small cruiser had to pay for 25 miles towage in order to avoid spending the night outside the shipping lane waiting for a favourable tide and wind.

If somebody gets into a really dangerous situation (as for

example running aground and incapable of getting afloat on their own and asks a RNLI vessel for assistance he should bear in mind that although the British RNLI does not charge for towing the lifeboat *crew* may make a charge so it is best to agree this before the rescue commences. One should also remember the calculation for the *Golden Years* which was only for a simple 'towage on the hook', the simplest way of being towed; the German lifeboat's towage fee is a minimum of 325 DM (£130) (depending on the size of the boat). This association, which is mainly financed from charities (mostly from people who take part in water sports), excuses its demands by stating: 'We only charged for the fuel consumption. Commercial companies would charge a substantially higher amount but we are not allowed to compete with them'.

According to the statutes of the British RNLI their prime aim is the rescue of life but will offer technical assistance like towing in and 'towing off when run aground' when called in by the Coastguard to assist.

You should try to get afloat by using your own resources and all other means available on board before calling another boat, for you are unlikely to know exactly what tariffs they will use to calculate the 'technical assistance' costs. Paying about £800 for assistance may not seem expensive if the owner can claim the money back from his insurance company. If he was to pay the first £400 himself (excess on his insurance policy) it may work out costly, especially if he loses his 'no claims bonus' which will add to the cost of his insurance in subsequent years.

It is also advisable to consider the wording and technical terms when agreeing on outside help for a grounded yacht: *towing off* is characterised as a special form of towing ie to tow a grounded yacht off an obstruction and get her afloat. This means *towing clear* until the boat reaches free water. In most cases the rescued boat will remain there for a while in order to clear all the lines which have been used. Sometimes the boat may need to anchor there to find out whether any damage has occurred before it continues its trip under its own power. It may need to ask for the second type of assistance: to be *towed in* to the nearest harbour if it is restricted in its manoeuvrability due to the grounding. The second type of assistance does not necessarily follow the first type and the possible payment for assistance may be evaluated completely differently.

One should also carefully consider which visual signals to display when asking for assistance for a grounded yacht and not assume a rescuer will come purely out of kindness. Signals like furious arm waving will be interpreted as emergency signals and described as such should the incident come to court. Waving with a rope is the best most non-committal request for friendly assistance in a non-emergency situation which might be resolved without outside help.

Emergency signals like waving your arms up and down or a MAYDAY call on the emergency frequency (VHF Channel 16) will automatically result in the highest compensation claims from the helper even if the situation is not dangerous.

Obviously, one should be towed with one's own gear for as long and as far as possible. Legally, and also from a financial aspect, it is irrelevant whose warps are used. If the larger boat prefers to work with its stronger and more durable warps to free the boat one can accept this decision without hesitation in the interest of a faster and safer rescue. What matters most is whether the crew of the grounded yacht is able to fasten the warp properly on their own or whether the helper is required to come aboard for this. Also of importance is whether the crew of the grounded yacht goes aboard the assisting boat before starting to get their yacht afloat; the helpers, therefore, have to work on an abandoned yacht. In this case, *assistance* can easily turn into *salvage* with all its resultant financial and legal consequences.

Salvage or *salvaging* are very important nautical and legal terms. Their usual meaning is 'to rescue' or 'bring to safety', but in connection with vessels and equipment it is only used if the owner has either given up his vessel or his equipment by his own free will or if the vessel is in peril. The difference between a *salvage charge* and a *charge for assistance* has both legal and financial implications. The crew of an assisting boat is entitled to both payments. Even professional salvagers are only entitled to claim a payment for assistance if the crew of the grounded yacht is on board during the freeing process. With friendly seamanship, as for example when help is given by another yachtsman, the compensation might only be the fuel consumption and the (possibly) damaged warps. A professional salvager may declare his costs as 'rescue of objects' or 'technical assistance' (as with the *Golden Years*) and therefore bill the recipient accordingly. They are also entitled to claim for damage on their vessel which occurred during the assistance although these amounts need to be reasonable. Neither the size or the value of the yacht which is freed *should* have influence on the amount of the assistance charge. A crew loses all rights of ownership if they abandon their grounded boat because they consider it to be too dangerous to remain on board in swell and surf or because the professional salvager has suggested that the crew come aboard his vessel in order to have a safer trip. They will only receive their yacht back (after being towed off successfully) if they pay the salvage charge; this depends on the value of the rescued (salvaged) boat and can be up to a third of its value ie a five or even six-figure sum.

If a fishing boat or another commercial vessel helps a yacht to get afloat, the grounded boat should agree on a charge beforehand and under no circumstances leave their yacht during the process. If the helper does not agree to this arrangement, a contract should be made with a professional salvager on the basis of 'no cure, no pay' which is in agreement with the 'Open Form' as suggested by yacht insurance companies. It can be verbally agreed between the two skippers and becomes effective when the assistance starts, whereby it is irrelevant who hands over the warp. If such contracts containing unreasonable clauses are drawn up at the place of the incident with the skipper under the pressure of a dangerous situation, it can later be declared invalid in court if the contract was deemed unreasonable. If there is a disagreement and a claim goes to court it may take years to settle as the insurers argue amongst themselves.

Dangers of stranding

Every year more yachts are stranded than generally supposed. There are numerous causes, some of which are quite unbelievable. Not only do boats go aground on sandy beaches but also on rocky coastlines where refloating may be very difficult and hazardous. If the crew acts correctly when the boat is stranded or beached, it very rarely means a total loss. The fact that yachts which have been abandoned in high seas may become beached after having drifted for days on end without a crew, and remain nearly undamaged, proves the old seafaring rule – if a boat is damaged or in danger of sinking during a coastal passage, the skipper should look for a place to beach his boat rather than give up and abandon ship.

Owners must always be prepared for the fact that their boats can go aground even when moored in so called protected harbours. A good example was the stranding of a huge number of cruisers and motor boats on the night of 27/28 August 1989 during the unexpected summer hurricane which hit marinas in the area of the Kieler Foorde in the Baltic. The narrow tongue of land used for protecting the mooring pontoons from the sea turned out to be inadequate as a safe breakwater when it was lashed by high seas driven by storm force onshore winds. The water level became so high in the harbour, that mooring lines were lifted off stern posts in the rising water. Yachts drifted towards the quay pulling other boats, which were still attached, with them. Damage compensation was only paid out on individual comprehensive insurance policies. Uninsured owners could not make use of their personal liability insurance for any damage because hurricanes are excluded from any claims due to the 'natural disaster' clause. These people not only lost their boat but they also had to pay for the wreckage to be removed.

Mass strandings like this can occur in any sailing area as

for example during the night of 6 December 1982 at the anchorage Cabo San Lucas at the southern tip of the Baja California in the Pacific. Due to a wind shift, which was totally unexpected at that time of the year, an onshore gale hit very suddenly. Most crews were totally unprepared and 28 large cruisers 'of an average length of 12 m and about 15 tonne displacement' were thrown on to the beach. Of these yachts, 22 were a total loss.

More yachts would have survived this disaster if drifting yachts had not dragged over other anchors and taken some of the safely anchored yachts with them. Similarly, the disaster would not have been as great had the stranded yachts been on their own on the beach and other yachts not been thrown on to them.

The main causes of stranding

Running aground may be caused by a natural disaster like a hurricane, typhoon or tropical cyclone which hits with little warning and throws the crew with their badly damaged yachts on to a beach. The majority of strandings are, however, caused by crew error.

Some singlehanded sailors habitually hand over the steering to the autopilot during the night so they can go down below to sleep. During this time they may be unaware of any dangerous wind shifts in coastal areas which could put the yacht on rocks or on a beach. They can be grateful that they have merely lost their yacht due to their lack of vigilance but have survived the stranding unharmed (Photo on page 53).

One finds it hard to be sympathetic when someone loses a boat because the whole crew went down below for a sleep at dusk with the boat close to islands, totally ignoring the danger of a wind shift and the tides.

There are also crews who anchor on a lee shore, then go to bed without an anchor watch, only waking up when their boat

This yacht was stranded during a passage because it was sailing on autopilot and the sleeping single-handed sailor did not realise there had been a dangerous windshift: The *Gipsy Moth* on the rocks in front of Gabor Island. The skipper, Desmond Hampton, was saved.

Stranded on a lee shore. Because they had no anchor watch and were fast asleep, the crew did not feel that the anchor was dragging on a dangerous anchorage.

is lying on a pebble beach in front of the promenade (See photo above).

Corner cutting often causes stranding as crews find themselves caught up in fishing nets. A poorly selected course along shallow coastlines, or a crippled engine when rounding a headland too close, can sometimes beach a boat because the crew did not use the anchor or the sails early enough as an alternative.

An important rule when entering or leaving port, especially when sailing close to a lee shore, is to run the engine whilst getting the sails ready ie make sure that the engine is going to function. Engine failure is a common cause of strandings.

Simple navigational errors may have far reaching consequences, as for example approaching a harbour from an unknown position at sea (see photo on page 55) or selecting the wrong lights when approaching a harbour at night.

In the interests of safety, one can be thankful if a boat

This yacht was stranded because the helmsman did not pay attention when entering his home port. The boat drifted into the surf right alongside the pierhead on a lee shore whilst under engine with the wind and the swell from abaft.

grounds 'gently' following a string of unlucky circumstances like the incident illustrated by the photo on page 56 when a yacht drifted on to a lee shore when hove-to during a gale. Another dangerous situation is if the anchor warp snaps whilst trying to hold a yacht with a damaged rudder and then the auxiliary rudder fails in the surf or if a cruiser cannot be tacked free after losing the anchor because the tiller or wheel is jammed. Another dangerous procedure is to run into harbour in high seas and onshore winds. If there is a bar in front of the entrance the keel may crash into it, causing the yacht to broach and become stranded. Also, a yacht is on a drying mooring in tidal waters, high onshore seas could smash the boat into wreckage on a nearby beach.

It is not only gross negligence, tropical cyclones or other spectacular circumstances like the incidents previously described that are the main causes of stranding. There are

Stranded on the westerly part of a North Sea beach on the island of Juist. The tide carried the hove-to yacht in the direction of the dangerous lee shore during a north westerly gale.

also simpler explanations like the common mistake of wrongly identifying lights during night passages causing a boat to run aground on shallows; tidal drifts can be calculated wrongly or not taken into account or the marks of narrow winding channels can be mixed up. Strandings can also be caused by dead reckoning errors in bad visibility (fog) or panic when approaching harbour perhaps brought on by lack of sleep and exhaustion, or wrong reading or error which was undetected on the compass, GPS or other navigational instruments. There is of course always danger from the sea state, tide and wind which even the best skipper is not immune to and only experience will tell you the best action to take.

Preparing for an intentional grounding

Situations may arise which make it necessary to run close in to the shore to look for a suitable place to beach a yacht gently so that the crew can be saved and severe damage to the boat can be avoided. This situation may have been caused by damage to the hull at sea with the boat taking in water or a leak caused by collision which potentially could sink the vessel if the bilge pumps were out of action.

If a yacht becomes disabled near the coast in onshore winds on a rising tide, the skipper may need to find a safe spot for beaching. He may have lost his rudder during a coastal passage or suffered damage to the steering gear. Other problems may include rope round the prop, an unreliable engine, damage to the rigging, ripped sails or a broken mast. Any one of these mishaps may be sufficient reason to plan to beach a boat as safely as possible. It may be the only alternative to a total loss at sea or getting shipwrecked at an inhospitable place and putting the crew in danger.

To start with, the skipper can choose the least dangerous area from the chart (Fig 36). The best choices are small bays whose inner reaches offer better protection against the in-coming swell than long coastlines because the outer edges act like breakwaters. The depth contour lines in these bays are important: Bay A and B show different underwater contours. A is the bay with the largest area of shoal water giving a short, choppy sea due to the shallow depth. This would be a suitable place to try and secure the yacht by using the anchor (Fig 37A). Bay B, on the other hand, has deeper water giving higher breaking waves and the actual beach is a lot narrower and more dangerous than A.

A shallow sandy beach also has the advantage that the grounding process can be gradual and the position of the yacht

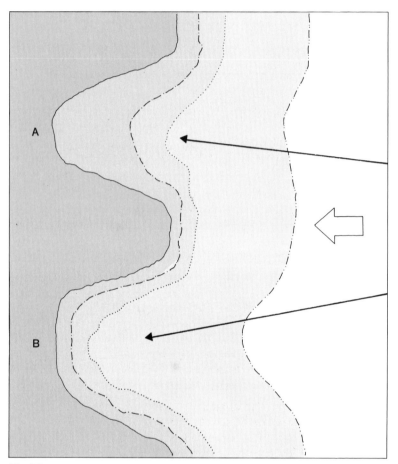

Fig 36

can be better controlled from the start. Another aspect to consider is whether the beached yacht should be towed back into deep water again after the repairs have been done or whether it should be lifted by crane and transported by road. (Most charts will also display roads that are adjacent to the coast.)

For a 'gentle' beaching it is important to release the anchor as quickly as possible so it can get a good hold. This can be done by backing up the second or kedge anchor by using its

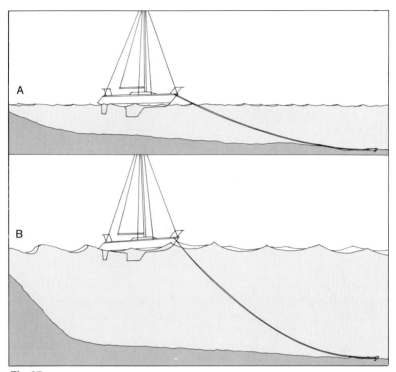

Fig 37

chain or a short warp to attach it to the main anchor (Fig 38,1) and lowering both anchors into the water about 10 m away (depending on the depth expected at the entrance of the bay). This length of chain will be secured with a light line on the foredeck which can break once the kedge has touched the bottom. The remaining anchor chain is laid out ready to run. If the windlass is used, the stopper knot on the chain needs to be released. Once the kedge starts to grip (Fig 38,2) the main anchor will also touch the bottom. The line will break and the complete anchor chain can run freely and both anchors should then hold at once and without the likelihood of the yacht's snubbing action breaking them out. The backed-up anchors and chain which lies as close as possible to horizontal, will achieve the best possible holding power (Fig 38,3). If this

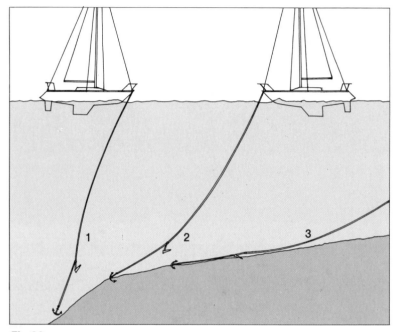

Fig 38

method is used you may be able to avoid beaching.

It can be quite risky to use only one anchor as it might not hold in a strong tide. Even if it holds, by the time the kedge is laid (if this is possible in high seas), the yacht will have moved much closer to the beach. If a yacht is taking water, the chain needs to be let out fast and, if necessary, the anchor warp attached until the boat is gently beached. Once the yacht is stranded, the skipper needs to decide whether the anchor should hold the bow towards the sea so the stern and rudder can dig into the sand or whether the boat should be turned into a different final position. This also depends on the hull configuration – a rudder which is not hung to the keel or supported by a skeg would probably break immediately. Once the weather has calmed down and the damage is sorted out, the crew stand a fair chance of being able to haul the yacht back to their anchor at the next high water springs.

What to do when your boat is high and dry

First of all, the boat must be brought into a position where it is best protected from further damage. A keelboat will always turn over to windward, ie towards the sea if it is stranded on a steep sandy beach. This makes the deck and its superstructure vulnerable to the breaking waves. In shallow water, keelboats always turn to leeward, ie towards the land. Each wave lifts the boat and repeatedly drops the leeside on to the beach which eventually leads to hull damage.

Using a similar method to that used to free a boat from an obstruction, the crew needs to heel the yacht towards the position that the skipper has chosen by swinging out the boom as a lever. Weight on the end of the boom or ropes which are attached at the crosstrees and led further away on the shore (as in Fig 22A) will help to keep the yacht in this position.

The hull should be protected with some sort of padding if possible which will cushion the unavoidable lifting and dropping movement of the wave action. Fenders, mattresses, sailbags

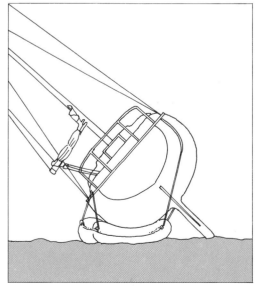

Fig 39

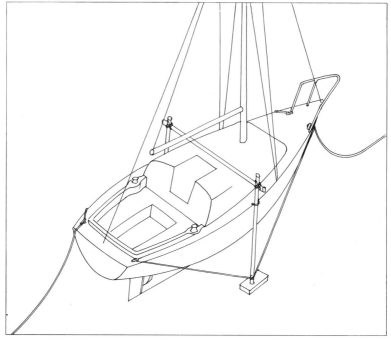

Fig 40

and even the inflated dinghy should be laid under the widest part of the boat from the turn of the bilge line to the gunwhale (Fig 39) and tied on securely.

If a boat is stranded on a pebbly beach or on a rocky coast, protection will be even more important and also more difficult. The best way, with a light boat, is to right it until it stands on an even keel, preventing it from falling back on to the rocks. To right the boat one should use the methods described for freeing a boat from an obstruction by using ground tackle (see page 15). Based on practical experience, this will prove to be quite difficult especially if the boat is already lying on one side in shallow water but it is essential to try it if you want to avoid further expensive damage.

Side supports (Fig 40) need to be built for righting a heavier boat on to an even keel. For this one can use all the available spars such as the main boom, spinnaker boom, boat hook, interior wood or anything available on board. These supports need to be lashed together with rope or steel cables at the top and fastened to a stanchion or other secure fitting on the gunwale. Pieces of wood or other flat panels should be placed underneath the spars to prevent them from sinking into sand or shingle. Finally, a warp should be passed round the hull and supports to keep the whole structure stable. To secure the boat safely from wind and waves one anchor should be rowed or waded out seaward as far as possible and the other one positioned abaft. You should try to turn the boat so the bow points out to sea so that the stern with its vulnerable rudder and the open cockpit point towards the shore. Even if the incoming waves lift the boat and bang the keel on the bottom it is better than suffering wave action abeam.

If a boat is stranded in deeper water, and the overturned boat overrun by the sea, it can easily be broken by the force of the breakers and quickly destroyed. If you think your boat is in danger of being broken up by large waves the best course of action is to 'sink' her. Lay out the anchors and shift any weight so that the overturned boat remains in position (Fig 41) and does not right itself simply in order to be knocked down again with the next wave. Then fill the water tanks with sea water to weigh down the hull. Experienced skippers flood the boat completely by opening all seacocks and leaving the hatches battened down. Obviously, this will ruin the engine but, due to the additional water ballast the boat is kept in a stable position on the seabed and hopefully can be salvaged.

The most important task is to secure the boat at the site of the stranding. On a shallow beach, carry the kedge anchor up the beach and dig it in firmly. Then row the heaviest (bower) anchor and another auxiliary from the quarters to seaward.

The position of the stranded yacht will decide whether it can be towed off by the sea or retrieved from the shore. If the boat is to be towed off, the crew should dig a channel and clear stones and other detritus at low water.

One crew member should stay on the beach to guard the yacht and maintain ownership to avoid the boat becoming

Fig 41

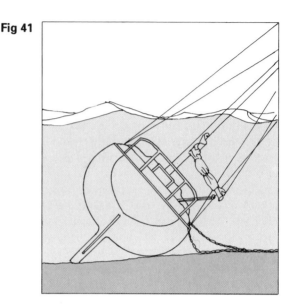

subject to Receiver of Wreck jurisdiction or the ravages of freelance salvage experts!

According to the Merchant Shipping Act of 1894, a wreck should be reported to the Receiver of Wreck (usually the local Coastguard or Customs officer) even by the owner who is in possession of it. The Receiver of Wreck claims possession of stranded yachts that have been abandoned by their crews. The owner of a stranded yacht is only liable for the value of the wreck for disposal purposes. If the cost of disposing of the wreck is larger than the value of the stranded yacht, the council responsible for the beach have to pay for the disposal. If this is the case the owner has to give up his rights to the stranded yacht by declaring it in writing to the Receiver of Wreck.

Stranding on quays

One imagines that a yacht would be safe in the shelter of a marina or harbour – this is not necessarily the case. Exposed harbours may present considerable risk. It is a dreadful feeling to watch helplessly as yachts are thrown on to quaysides and virtually split open before they sink or are even thrown bodily over the quay wall on to the adjacent road! If a boat lies alongside a stone pier and the harbour is exposed to the sea or to a bay (even if it is narrow), it can easily become endangered by onshore winds and incoming swell. The boat lifts and drops in the choppy sea and constantly bangs against the harbour wall. The fenders may offer little protection as they are jerked out of position. The following rescue methods can be used if the boat cannot clear the danger zone under engine.

Get the dinghy ready (or ask the crew of a small motor boat for help) and drive out the main anchor sideways from the pier and in the direction of wind and sea on a very long scope (Fig 42). Make sure that the anchor warp does not interfere with other traffic (for example ferries). You can also lower another heavy anchor to the bottom on a separate warp. The anchor warp is then secured amidships and the boat pulled towards the anchor; this gives a safe clearance from the quayside.

If necessary, two warps can be secured to the anchor leading to bow and stern, holding the boat parallel to the quay. To achieve an additional cushioning effect, the two-part anchor

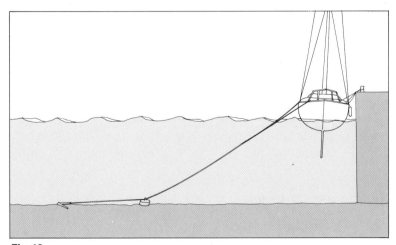

Fig 42

warp is secured on the lee side of the boat (towards the quay) to secure fittings such as sheet winches and shroud plates (Fig 43B). Another method of stabilising the boat at the quay is to drop a warp round the keel (Fig 43A). The problem with this is a risk of chafe, so a double warp would be safer. If enough anchor gear is onboard one should use both methods.

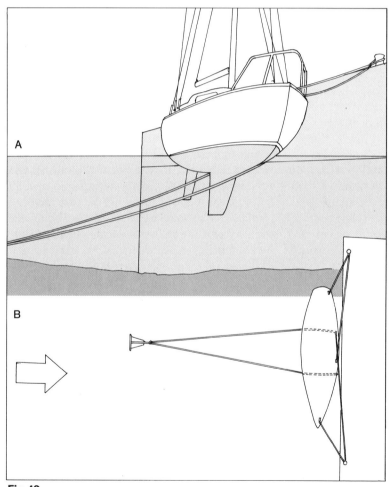

A

B

Fig 43

Salvaging stranded yachts

In earlier days, the word 'stranding' nearly always meant a total loss and therefore a wreck. Most traditional heavy wooden boats were damaged to such an extent when they smashed against the shore that they virtually broke apart and there was nothing to save; or if they were lucky and stayed in one piece they were too heavy to be transported by road. Transport facilities did not exist in those days. The invention of the light displacement cruiser in the 1950's made it possible for small cruisers to survive a stranding, not only largely undamaged but also capable of being transported by land.

The earliest yacht I know of to be beached by its crew in order to prevent total loss and to save their lives was the *Tilly Twin*, 10.7 m long, 2.65 m wide and with a draught of 2.13 m. In the summer of 1956 a hurricane struck 23 yachts between 27 and 29 July that were taking part in a 220 mile offshore race crossing the channel from England to France. The crew of the *Tilly Twin* were driven towards the coast near Portsmouth. At first they tried to stop the yacht drifting onshore by using the method described in Fig 37 but when they saw the option of beaching the boat quickly and with less danger on a clear beach and at higher water rather than smashing it on rocks at low water, they slipped warp and anchor so the yacht could quickly drift across the rocky barrier. The keel bounced lightly off the rocks about a dozen times until the boat was lying almost horizontal. It then drifted on to the beach with the keel dragging over the bottom like an anchor until she came to rest in about a metre of water. After the boat was secured it was checked for damage. This turned out to be only superficial which astonished the crew who were uninjured. A few days later the *Tilly Twin* was craned on to a low loader and put back into the water at her home port.

What was a sensation in those days is now quite a common occurrence – the rescue of boats of 10 or even 15 tonne displacement in an emergency is not so unusual.

This 12 m short-keel light displacement yacht (above and opposite) was rescued with difficulty from the sandy beach on Fuerteventura. A front loader had to move close in to the high side of the yacht and carefully dig out the sand near the fin keel at low water. The yacht could then be lifted at the bow and turned over on to its port side. The towing warp was then secured to the keel like a harness in front and abaft the fin and the cruiser was pulled, stern first, into the sea until it was back afloat. The cost of the releasing and towing operation and the repair for the damage to the gel coat on the outer hull was within a reasonable limit, though the strong salvage tug which was chartered was fairly expensive and had a long return journey.

Running aground and getting afloat

The 12 m GRP yacht was safely beached on soft sand and towed off by a powerful tug from a nearby harbour. It was fortunate that the yacht had a bilge keel to which the heavy towing warp could be secured. This is the best point to absorb the immense strain put on the hull when towing off a beach.

The 9 m fin-keeled steel cruiser survived a stranding at high water in the soft sand of a North Sea island with damage only to the rudder and the skeg. A caterpillar digger and a crane were brought to the island to rescue the yacht. A ditch was dug on the starboard side to right the boat which was then lifted and slowly slung across the dunes ready for subsequent transport by road and ferry. ▼

Running aground and getting afloat

▲ This cruiser was stranded on a reef whilst entering the harbour of Barcadera on Aruba at night. The harbour light, which marks the harbour entrance (poorly at the best of times) was unlit and the skipper made a disastrous approach.

Before the yacht was towed off, she was lifted off the rocks with buoyancy bags which allowed the boat to be pulled into deeper water without further damage to the hull.

◀ Unsuccessful rescue attempts to free a 9 m GRP cruiser. First, a small fishing vessel tried to tow the cruiser off into deep water from the pebbly beach; this proved unsuccessful. Then a front loader started working from the shore. It pulled the 3 ton cruiser further on to the pebbly beach so that eventually the bow touched the curb on the road causing further damage. A strong tug could have rescued the yacht with less damage whilst it was still stranded in deeper water.

Summary of rescue methods

It is possible to tow off a stranded yacht from a sandy beach into the sea with hardly any damage. Towing off from pebbly ground or rocks nearly always leads to further damage to the boat. Before starting the rescue work, the path to the water needs to be cleared of all stones including those buried in the sand. To make the procedure easier, a short narrow channel for the keel (the fin must be cleared) needs to be dug at low water because towing off must be carried out at high water. If possible, a ballast keel should be detached (There are at least 6 to 10 bolts attaching a keel to the hull of a modern cruiser). The openings should be made as watertight as possible.

Small fishing boats and motor cruisers may not have sufficient engine power to tow a large yacht free. You might have to charter a special salvage vessel but the increased cost is well worth it. The towing warp can either be secured by rigging the tackle like a harness around the hull (Fig 32), attaching straps which are tied around the hull laterally (see photo on page 68) or by putting the warp around the upper edge of the fin (see photo on page 70). Even the strongest fittings will not hold the immense strain during the towing procedure.

JCBs, hydraulic cranes and other types of construction machinery that can drive to the stranded yacht are the best way of digging out and lifting the boat. The machinery can also transport the boat to a road. The photo on page 71 shows a yacht with its mast taken down being lifted by a crane. Success of the procedure obviously largely depends on the suitability of the access roads.

An ideal but also quite expensive means of assistance is a floating crane which can be towed in from a nearby harbour. Because of its shallow draught it can be anchored close enough to the beach so that its cantilever jib reaches the stranded yacht. Once the yacht is retrieved it can be loaded on to the crane and transported to a boatyard for repair.

If a rescued yacht remains largely undamaged and small leaks can be quickly plugged, she can be swung back into deeper water so that she can be towed to a boatyard for repair.

Even if a yacht has run aground on a reef and a crane is unable to get close enough to free it because of dangerous shallows, the boat still need not become a wreck. These days, reputable salvage firms possess large inflatable buoyancy bags, made from very tough rubber, which are placed under the hull to free the yacht. With the aid of portable compressors these bags can be inflated on the stranded yacht itself and also serve to keep a leaking yacht buoyant once she has reached deeper water (See photo on page 73).

However, be warned: a rushed rescue can lead to more damage than that already caused by the grounding. Because of this, the stranded yacht might be damaged beyond repair. So make sure that the rescue is carried out by professionals using the correct methods and equipment.

If a stranded yacht is in little danger of being further damaged by bad weather or a rising tide, you should check out all possible options before starting to rescue the boat. Obviously, you must contact your insurance company which will send an agent who will make a decision at the scene of the incident.

Signals when aground

A yacht which is fast aground will want to display (in her own interest and in order to gain assistance from other pleasure craft or commercial vessels in her vicinity) that she has run aground. According to Collision Regulations, she must display the appropriate signals day and night. She should also provide information about the imminent danger before she runs aground or strands.

Warnings and seeking assistance on VHF radio

A yacht which is in danger of running aground, or has run aground near a shipping lane or a deep water channel, has to contact the Coastguard on the emergency channel (VHF channel 16) using the Securité prefix. By sending this safety warning the skipper alerts other skippers to potential danger in their vicinity so that they can reduce speed when passing the grounded yacht in order to lessen their bow wave and stern wake. A Securité message is not a request for assistance!

Assistance is sought by using the international PAN PAN code. By repeating the words PAN three times, the calling station announces that it wants to send an urgent message which relates to the boat. This message has priority over all other calls with the exception of the distress call MAYDAY. PAN PAN indicates that the stranded or grounded boat is in danger but the life of the crew is not at risk. The skipper can ask the coastal station, or other vessels which receive the message, for assistance to get afloat or may request for replacement parts to be made available, so that the yacht can free itself once the necessary repair work has been done.

The international distress call MAYDAY should only be

used if the yacht is in immediate danger and the life of the crew is at risk. This rarely happens when boats run aground unless the yacht is lying in tidal waters with very high seas running or if the boat is stranded on a rocky coastline and the crew is unable to reach the shore without risking their lives or getting injured. It would be irresponsible to send a MAYDAY call to ask the Coastguard for assistance to tow off a yacht which is not in danger simply because the crew want to save themselves effort and intend to claim their expenses through their insurance company.

Daytime visual and sound signals

If a yacht is in danger of running aground in heavy weather or is drifting on to a coastline with a dragging anchor she should, if possible, hoist the flag 'Yankee' which, in accordance with the International Signalling Code, means: 'I am dragging my anchor'. The red and yellow diagonally striped flag serves two purposes: it alerts other crews close by to your situation so that they can help to prevent your boat from running aground or stranding. It also warns them of the danger that your anchor can foul their anchors causing them also to go adrift.

In accordance with the International Regulations For Preventing Collisions At Sea, the most important rule for the skipper to observe when his boat is aground is Rule 30:

Rule 30

Anchored vessels and vessels aground
    (a) A vessel at anchor shall exhibit where it can best be seen:
        (i) in the fore part, an all round white light or one ball;
        (ii) at or near the stern and at a lower level than the light prescribed in sub paragraph (i), an all round white light.
    (b) A vessel of less than 50 metres in length may exhibit an

all-round white light where it can best be seen instead of the lights prescribed in paragraph (a) of this Rule.

(c) A vessel at anchor may, and a vessel of 100 metres and more in length shall, also use the available working or equivalent lights to illuminate her decks.

(d) A vessel aground shall exhibit the lights prescribed in paragraph (a) or (b) of this Rule and in addition, where they can best be seen:

(i) two all round red lights in a vertical line;

(ii) three balls in a vertical line.

(e) A vessel of less than 7 metres in length, when at anchor not in or near a narrow channel, fairway or anchorage, or where other vessels normally navigate, shall not be required to exhibit the lights or shape prescribed in paragraphs (a) and (b) of this Rule.

(f) a vessel of less than 12 metres in length, when aground, shall not be required to exhibit the lights or shapes prescribed in sub paragraphs (d) (i) and (ii) of this Rule.

If grounded by night or day you need to observe Rule 35:

Rule 35

(g) A vessel at anchor shall at intervals of not more than one minute ring the bell rapidly for about 5 seconds. In a vessel of 100 metres or more in length the bell shall be sounded in the forepart of the vessel and immediately after the ringing of the bell the gong shall be sounded rapidly for about 5 seconds in the after part of the vessel. A vessel at anchor may in addition sound three blasts in succession, namely one short, one prolonged and one short blast, to give warning of her position and of the possibility of collision to an approaching vessel.

(h) A vessel aground shall give the bell signal and if required the gong signal prescribed in paragraph (g) of this Rule and shall, in addition, give three separate and distinct strokes on the bell immediately before and after the rapid ringing of the bell. A vessel aground may in addition sound an appropriate whistle signal.

Small vessels under 12 metres only need to give a sound signal every two minutes. All these visual and sound signals are intended as a warning to other vessels. If the boat has no VHF radio or it is out of order and communicating with other boats by megaphone is impossible, important messages can be signalled to passing ships by hoisting two flag signals in accordance with the International Code Book. The flags 'Juliet Hotel' (Fig 44) are blue-white-blue horizontal and red-white vertical. This flag combination indicates: 'I have run aground. I am not in danger.' These can be hoisted to avoid unwanted helpers.

One can also avoid possible rescue attempts from other vessels, by hoisting 'Juliet Lima' (Fig 45). The second flag, 'Lima', is black and yellow chequered. Combined with Juliet it means: 'You are in danger of running aground'. You can hoist the flag 'Uniform' (Fig 47) which is chequered red and white. It indicates: 'You are running into danger'.

Fig 44

If help is required it can be displayed by hoisting flags 'Juliet Golf' (Fig 46), blue-white-blue horizontal and blue-yellow striped vertically. This combination says 'I have run aground. I am in a dangerous situation'. If the skipper has difficulty steering the boat once she is afloat again and is drifting into a shipping lane or a busy anchorage, the single flag 'Delta' (Fig 48) is hoisted which indicates: 'Keep clear of me. I am manoeuvring with difficulty.' Knowledge of the code flags may be useful but you are likely to be preoccupied with more important jobs once the boat is back afloat, than hoisting signal flags.

Fig 45

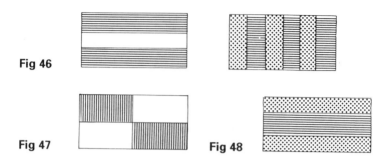

Fig 46

Fig 47   **Fig 48**

Also you may not have a full set of flags on board. It is a good idea, however, to give signals as soon as possible in accordance with the Collision Regulations, especially if you are likely to become involved with an insurance claim.

Visual and sound signals at night

At night, a grounded yacht over 12 metres in length needs to display its anchor light (Rule 30(a) and (b) of the Collision Regulations) and additionally two red all-round lights (Rule 30(d)). Smaller cruisers and motorboats do not have to comply with these rules. The law assumes that these boats, because of their shallow draught, only run aground in areas that are not close to the deep water channels or shipping lanes and therefore do not represent a danger to large vessels.

Drying areas

Along coasts, affected by tidal waters, are wide areas of shallows that dry out at low water and are flooded again at high water. On modern charts, waters down to a 10 metre depth contour line are printed in light blue. Areas which dry at low water are shown in green. All depths given on charts are the depths of water below chart datum (the lowest astronomical tide).

Drying out

Drying out can also be an intentional grounding of a yacht on an outgoing tide. It is generally done on a soft bottom. The yacht will be high and dry and one can virtually walk around her. In tidal harbours that are only accessible in a rising tide or at high water, all boats will dry out once the tide ebbs. The crew can use this time to work on the exposed part of the hull below the water line. A tide table gives the skipper information about the tidal range and the time for high and low water and therefore the period of time in which the yacht will be high and dry. The drying area might be large but not every part of it will by suitably for drying out. When selecting a suitable place you need to keep away from sandbanks pointing seawards or to areas that are reached by swell. In bad weather the boat should not be allowed to dry out on mud close to the inner edges of creeks because the incoming tide can develop a ground swell in these areas.

If you want your yacht to dry out it should be motored from deep water into a creek and positioned over the mudflats. Then turn the boat against the wind and drop the anchor in the chosen position. Not all boats are suitable for drying out in open areas of mudflats. If you intend sailing in shallow waters and drying out in tidal harbours you should choose a bilge keeler (with two keels or three if there is an additional centre keel) or a centreboarder or lifting keel; alternatively a displacement yacht that has a shallow draught with a bilge keel is also suitable. All large keel boats, especially fin keelers, are unsuitable for sailing in shallow waters and drying out, even if they can be propped up with supports which protect them from falling on to their sides.

Multihulls can also stand upright without support so are suitable for drying out. A boat with a deep draught can also dry out in tidal harbours if it is positioned so that it can be

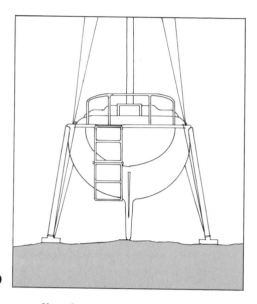

Fig 49

supported by the harbour wall at low tide; make sure that the hull is well protected by fenders. A bilge keeler or bilge keeler with a centre keel are typical shallow water boats. They are constructed to stand upright when drying out because of their short twin, stumpy keels which are attached on either side of the underwater hull. With a V-bottomed boat the short keels (slightly splayed, sometimes without ballast) are attached to the heavy internal stringers or underwater hull which prevent them from pressing in or through the thin hull if the boat is heeled when dried out and the load is resting on only one keel. A centreboarder like a fin keeler can dry out with additional supports. These can either be propped under the side of the gunwale (on smaller boats, Fig 49) and secured once the yacht has touched bottom or are connected on each side to a pivoting chain plate. The supports can also be made to include built in steps which make it easier to get on and off the boat. For people who regularly sail over shallows which dry out every day, the supports can be attached to the boat with swivels so they can be lowered when needed. When the boat is underway these supports are secured horizontally along the

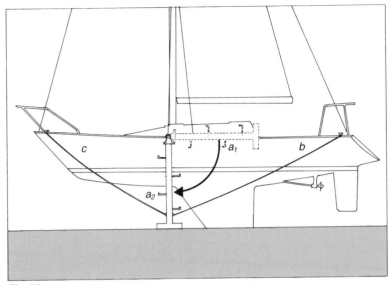

Fig 50

topsides below the gunwale. As the tide goes out, and shortly before the yacht touches bottom, the supports are lowered (Fig 50 Position a_1 to a_2) until it is vertical next to the keel. The lines for the uphaul (b) and the downhaul (c) are secured abaft on the foredeck. These lines prevent possible collapse of the supports which would turn the yacht on its side. Supports can be used on all long keeled boats. The keel, however, needs to be of a sufficient length to prevent the boat pivotting on to bow or stern when people move on deck or down below (Fig 51). Due to the weight of the engine most yachts tend to drop lower at the stern in any case. Inevitably, this means that fin keelers are unsuitable or only have limited ability to sail over mud-flats. To hold the boat safely the supports need to be pointing upwards (Fig 52), not vertically to the ground. Swivelled supports are operated similarly to the leeboards on Thames barges or traditional Dutch sailing vessels. When beaching a boat in soft mud the feet of the supports should be fitted with base plates to give them a larger area to stand on.

Running aground and getting afloat

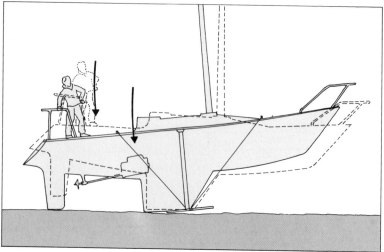

Fig 51

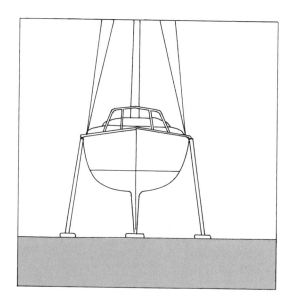

Fig 52

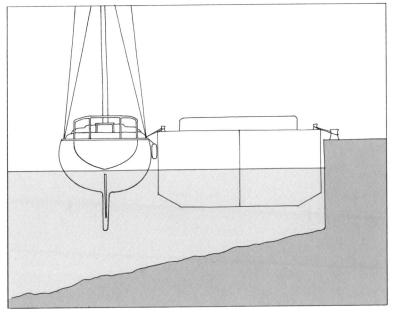

Fig 53

It is not generally necessary to anchor when drying out provided that the crew stays close to the boat and goes back on board when the tide comes in. If the chart shows an uneven formation of the ground or it is feared that the mudflat bottom (which can rarely be clearly identified from the boat) slopes upwards as it does at the landward end of a creek, you should use the main anchor and kedge to stay in position. With an incoming tide and cross wind the boat may be pushed sideways on to the slope and fall on its side. Obviously anchoring is essential when staying overnight with the tidal change in darkness or whilst the crew is asleep.

In tidal harbours one may decide to moor alongside a large commercial vessel. (Fig 53). The advantage is that your mooring lines do not require much checking when the water level changes but it is a very risky decision. If the bottom slopes away from the quay, a heavily loaded barge can end up lean-

Running aground and getting afloat

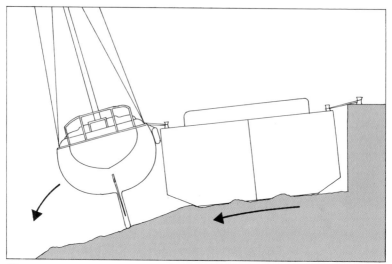

Fig 54

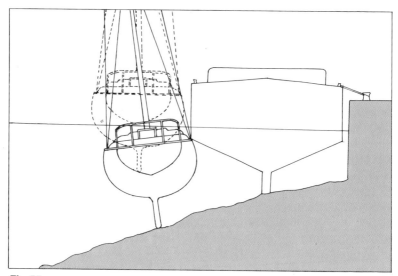

Fig 55

ing against the hull of your yacht which is prevented from sliding sideways because her keel is wedged into the mud (Fig 54). A fin keeler can be overturned in a situation like this.

If the large vessel has been lying there for a longish period of time, her keel will be well dug into the mud. On an outward sloping ground the yacht tied outside can slip with her guard rail or gunwale sliding under her neighbour's chine (Fig 55) wedging the boat under the surface and possibly flooding it. Even if not actually sunk it will inevitably have damaged its guard rail, side deck or even the shrouds.

Some tidal harbours have a small area of concrete next to

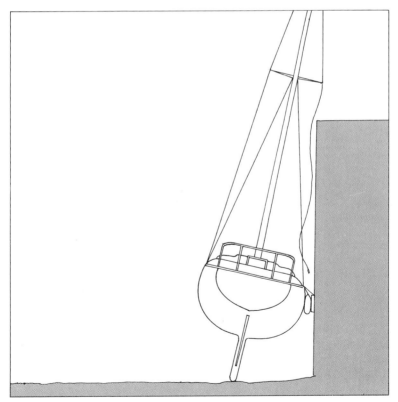

Fig 56

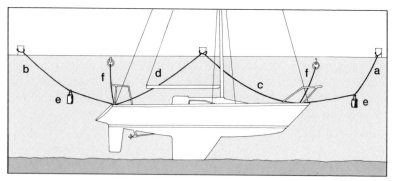

Fig 57

the harbour wall or quay which allows a boat to dry out without putting it in danger and at low water permits the crew to carry out repair work or paint the hull. When the yacht starts to dry out she should be turned slightly towards the harbour wall so she cannot fall the other way. The rigging should not touch the wall or any quayside structures when the yacht is lying dry or during the rising and falling tides. If the rigging does touch the harbour wall (Fig 56) during a falling tide, the turnbuckle of the shroud should be opened and the shroud taken off or the rigging should be loosened at the chain plate. During the outgoing tide the hull must remain in constant contact with the harbour wall, obviously well protected by fenders. If you decide that the heeling angle is insufficient and the boat will still try to fall the other way, the yacht can be secured by attaching a mastline from the spreaders to the quayside. The heeling angle can be helped by shifting ballast down below and on deck. Bow and stern lines (a and b in Fig 57) as well as fore and aft springs (c and d in Fig 57) should be secured to the quay. The springs should be of sufficient length to allow for the tidal range. To keep the boat under better control in high water, weights (e) can be attached halfway along the bow and stern lines; you can use anchor weights, a light kedge anchor or a piece of heavy chain.

Pulling the boat towards the quay at high water can be made easier if additional bow and stern lines are led almost vertically up the quayside and secured to a ring or bollard (f in Fig 57). In tidal harbours without jetties or piles where bilge keelers or centreboarders generally remain afloat even at low water, it is advisable to secure them with a long shore line and bring out a kedge anchor. This stops the boat from swinging into neighbouring boats. Here are a few important tips about mooring in drying areas:

● If anchoring is required in mudflats make sure that your main anchor is of the right type (CQR or Danforth) and weight to give good holding power in soft mud.

● For drying in harbours the boat should also be well equipped with fenders. Car tyres can be used against the harbour wall for added protection. Use a fender board between tyres and fenders to protect your gel coat or paintwork.

● When you arrive in a tidal harbour make inquiries as to whether the vacant mooring place at the quayside is suitable for drying. In particular ask whether the quay wall is straight and clean; if the ground is level or slopes away; whether you need to be careful of rubbish on the bottom and whether there are warning signs in the vicinity which need to be obeyed.

● If you tie up alongside another yacht you have to notify the other crew that you will dry out. Exchange information regarding your draughts. The boat with the shallower draught should always lie on the outside and slacken its lines once the inner boat has touched bottom. Otherwise, the bigger boat could fall towards the wall and jam the smaller boat against the harbour wall.

● The deck fairleads used for mooring need to be suitable for a near vertical pull. Use overlapping leads or close the lips with a rope end. The best mooring cleat is a bitt or a bollard with a cross bar. Stainless steel fairleads through which mooring lines are led off the deck, protect the lines and the hull during changes of tide.

● To protect the boat from falling away from the quay wall during the outgoing tide, a strong line should be rove through a block and hoisted between deck and masthead with a halyard. The block is then tied to a short, strong rope which is secured on a bollard or ring on the quay. This security line is self-adjusting in all tidal heights and maintains a constant distance from the mast to the quay wall.

● The bow and stern should also be supported if work needs to be done on the hull once the yacht has dried out. Support, similar to that used in dry docks, is essential for light short-keeled boats in order to keep them stable.

● The weather should also be monitored carefully when the yacht is dry. Strong offshore winds can push the yacht away from the quayside and heel her over if the mooring lines are slack.

Once afloat, whether you have dried out in a harbour or on mudflats, check anything which could be clogged up with mud. Check the inlet and outlet seacocks of the heads, cooling water inlet and outlet for the engine, drains in the galley, the bilges below deck and in the cockpit, bilge pump; and obviously check that the log and echo sounder are working.

Drying out is not that easy. The incoming tide can soon flood a badly secured boat if it is tipped over on its side. If all hints and tips you have gathered are observed, the fear of the first intended ground contact will soon be overcome and the pleasures of the isolation and peace of the mudflats and their abundant bird life will be appreciated.

Glossary

This short glossary gives a definition of terms which are briefly touched on in this book or might be of legal importance. A few other terms have been included which have not been mentioned in the book but might prove to be useful additional knowledge.

Bar is a sandbank which is close to the shore and lies parallel to a beach, a river estuary or a harbour entrance. It produces a ground swell or surf in heavy weather. Grounding only occurs in the trough of a wave. It is often possible to sail over a bar at high water whilst it remains impassable during low water.

Beaching or **stranding** not only applies to yachts stranded on beaches; it can mean being aground on shoals or obstructions of any kind. The yacht lies 'high and dry' and is incapable of freeing itself.

Disposal of wreck The expenditure for this is paid for by the owner or his insurance company. Disposal costs are limited to the value of the stranded yacht. A few years ago, the disposal of a wreck simply meant the removal of the unwanted boat from the place of where it was wrecked. Wooden boats were burned, steel boats dismantled and recycled as far as possible. The disposal of modern GRP boats creates a problem. According to the present regulations, GRP boats can be deposited on ordinary rubbish dumps if their hulls are cut into pieces. The insurance company will pay for disposal within the terms of a comprehensive insurance policy.

Getting afloat means to free a stranded boat from an obstruction with self-help measures or outside assistance.

Ground swell is a short, steep breaking wave produced by high swell from deep water running on to shallows like shoals, bars or sandbanks. It disturbs the bottom of the sea and carries sand or pebbles.

Lightening a boat is the first and most important measure to get it back afloat once grounded. Yachts can reduce their displacement ie. their draught when lightened. Fresh water supplies, tools and other heavy equipment should be transferred into a dinghy and, if necessary, some of the crew should also board the dinghy.

Receivers of Wreck are Crown Officers, usually Coast guards or Customs Officers to whom any wrecks have to be reported; they take responsibility for the wreck and its equipment and cargo.

Reef is a wide area of rocks that can be above the water level or lie underneath it. It is predominantly found in areas with rocky coastlines. In a swell the danger is clearly indicated by the breaking waves but if the sea is smooth the underwater dangers are often invisible or only visible from a close distance.

Scrapping is the dismantling and demolition of a wrecked boat. Scrapping for the purpose of disposing of a wreck can be a costly procedure which the insurance company usually pays for.

Stranded goods need to be reported to the local Receiver of Wreck. Stranded goods can consist of any kind of washed up items and, in addition, can include stranded yachts which are largely undamaged. These goods are subject to the jurisdiction of the Receiver of Wreck.

Tidal harbour is an open harbour which is only accessible at high water. Every moored boat is subject to the rise and fall of the tide. Boats moored at the quay or on buoys dry out in tidal harbours at low water.

Towing off is the term for towing a grounded boat off an obstruction into deep water.

Towing in describes towing a boat in deep water, for example a vessel that is restricted in its manoeuvrability, to the next harbour or safe anchorage.

Wreck is a grounded or stranded yacht which has been abandoned by its crew and is reported missing or unusable.

Wreckers are a danger for any stranded yacht. They are people who operate not only on beaches but also on shoals, bars, rocks etc which are accessible by boat.

Printed in Great Britain
by Amazon

39994441R00091